TWAYNE'S WORLD LEADERS SERIES

EDITOR OF THIS VOLUME

Samuel Smith, Ph.D.

Heinrich Pestalozzi

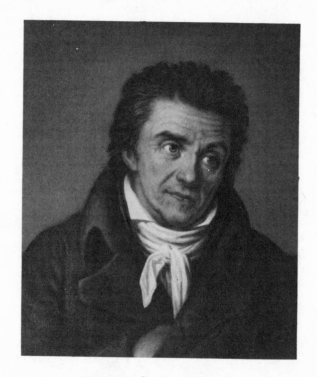

Heinrich Pestalozzi

Heinrich Pestalozzi

Father of Modern Pedagogy

By ROBERT B. DOWNS

TWAYNE PUBLISHERS
A DIVISION OF G. K. HALL & CO., BOSTON

471353

Library of Congress Cataloging in Publication Data

Downs, Robert Bingham, 1903-
  Heinrich Pestalozzi, father of modern pedagogy.

  (Twayne's world leaders series)
  Bibliography: p. 143.
  1. Pestalozzi, Johann Heinrich, 1746-1827.
LB627.D68   370'.92'4 [B]   74-14554
ISBN 0-8057-3560-7

Contents

About the Author

Robert B. Downs has directed three major university libraries: University of North Carolina, 1932-38, New York University, 1938-43, and the University of Illinois, 1943-71. As Dean of Library Administration at Illinois, he served as head of the University Library and of the Graduate School of Library Science.

Dean Downs has held numerous foreign assignments, under governmental and foundation sponsorship, in Japan, Mexico, Turkey, Afghanistan, Tunisia, Sweden, Canada, United Kingdom, and various South American countries, to establish libraries and library schools, to survey library resources and library education, and as special lecturer. He has served as First Vice President and President of the American Library Association, and President of the Association of College and Research Libraries. He holds honorary degrees from six institutions: Colby College, University of North Carolina, University of Toledo, Ohio State University, Southern Illinois University, and University of Illinois.

Among other honors, Dean Downs has received the Clarence Day Award, sponsored by the Association of American Publishers, in recognition of "substantial published work promoting a love of reading"; the Joseph W. Lippincott Award "for distinguished service in the profession of librarianship"; the Illinois Library Association's "Librarian of the Year Award"; Syracuse University's Centennial Medal; and a Guggenheim Foundation Fellowship.

Dean Downs is the author of numerous books and articles, including *Books That Changed the World* (translated into 12 languages), *Books That Changed America, Famous American Books, Molders of the Modern Mind, Famous Books Ancient and Medieval,* and *Horace Mann* (Twayne's Great Educators Series.)

Preface

Some years ago, in the preparation of a work published under the title *Molders of the Modern Mind* (N.Y. :Barnes & Noble, 1961), an attempt to identify and to analyze books which have been most influential in shaping Western culture, it soon became evident that the name of Heinrich Pestalozzi holds high rank. The development of elementary education over the past century and a half can hardly be understood without recognition of Pestalozzi's seminal role.

Further insight into the basic nature of Pestalozzi's contributions came in the writing of a biography of Horace Mann (N.Y.: Twayne Publishers Inc., 1974). Throughout Mann's remarkable educational career, the impact of Pestalozzi's concepts and theories stand out. Thus, we find Pestalozzian ideas transplanted to the public schools of Massachusetts and ultimately to North and South America. Even more direct was the profound impression on German education, exerted through the writings of Johann Gottlieb Fichte, Friedrich Frobel, Johann Friedrich Herbart, and others inspired by Pestalozzi's teachings.

The volume of writings relating to Pestalozzi is immense. The latest and most scholarly edition of his collected works, issued by the Pestalozzianum and Zentralbibliothek of Zurich, runs to twenty-one volumes, and a Japanese edition (further evidence of Pestalozzi international influence) totals some eighteen volumes. J. G. Klink's Pestalozzi bibliography for the period 1923-1965 contains 1,894 entries. A justification for adding to this large body of literature is that published references to Pestalozzi are predominantly in the German language and with a few exceptions—e.g., Silber, Heafford, Gutek, and Walch—there is a shortage of up-to-date studies in English. The present work has attempted also to incorporate the results of the most recent investigations and interpretations dealing with Pestalozzi's life and times, his educational theories and practices.

Particular acknowledgment should be made to three Swiss institutions for their aid in research during a period spent in Switzerland during the fall of 1973. These were the Pestalozzianum and Zentralbibliothek of Zurich and the Stadtbibliothek of Winterthur. The two libraries maintain extensive collections of works by and about Pestalozzi and the Pestalozzianum holds, in addition to a considerable book collection, numerous valuable artifacts and other museum-type materials which are helpful in gaining an understanding of Pestalozzi's varied activities.

Appreciation should also be expressed to Elizabeth C. Downs for her assistance in research for this work and to Deloris Holiman for the preparation of the manuscript.

Robert B. Downs

Chronology

1746   Born January 12, at Zurich, Switzerland. One of three surviving children of Johann Baptist and Susanna (Hotz) Pestalozzi.

1751   Death of father.

1754- Student in a Latin school and later in the Collegium
1765   Humanitatis and the Collegium Carolinum.

1767   Studied agriculture under Johann Rudolf Tschiffeli.

1768   Purchased and began operation of Neuhof farm.

1769   Married to Anna Schulthess.

1774- After failure of agriculture experiment, established school
1778   for poor children in Neuhof home.

1780- Period of greatest literary activity.
1798

1799   Institution for war orphans established at Stans, under Pestalozzi's management.

1799   Following forced closing of Stans orphanage, became elementary school teacher in Burgdorf.

1800- Directed school in Burgdorf Castle.
1804

1805- Established and directed experimental school at Yverdon.
1825

1815   Death of wife.

1825   Yverdon institute closed.

1827   Died February 17, at Brugg.

CHAPTER 1

Education Pre-Pestalozzian

UNTIL the coming of the Renaissance in Europe in the fifteenth century, the actual process of teaching had remained largely unmodified for nearly two thousand years. The underlying principle developed at Ptolemaic Alexandria in the third century B.C. and reigning supreme for centuries thereafter, was that the school exists to teach the written word. Important changes in the theory and practice of education emerged along with the great intellectual movement known as the Renaissance. Ideas became democratized. Learning was no longer a monopoly of the clergy and the church, but was now open to everyone who had sufficient ability, leisure, and means to pursue it.

After a long struggle, the spirit of the Renaissance spread over all of Western Europe and the traditional teaching of the higher schools and universities was forced to adapt itself to new and different demands. The spread of knowledge by way of the newly invented printing press from about 1450 onward broke the tight ecclesiastical grip on books which had prevailed throughout the medieval era. Scholarly activity was tremendously accelerated by the printers' prolific output. Greek studies were revived and the prose of Cicero, as a basis for the study of Latin, replaced the rhymed grammars that for hundreds of years had held sway in the schools. Through use of the printing press, one teacher was able to instruct thousands of students.

On the other hand, while the Renaissance did much to stimulate the intellectual life of the higher schools, its effects on education in general were less noticeable and to some extent were pernicious. The separation of the primary or lower schools from the universities and higher schools left a gulf that was not bridged until comparatively modern times.

Further changes occurred with the coming of the Reformation.

For Martin Luther, the elementary school was the center of concern. In his view, everyone must be able to read the Bible, and since the people in general were unable to understand the Latin version, the Bible was translated by Luther into the common tongue. The function of the school as conceived by Luther, however, was just as narrow as it had been in the medieval period. The school remained a servant of the church. All children, boys and girls, must learn to read the Bible and be taught the catechism Luther had written for them. In addition, the state should use its powers to compel neglectful parents to send their children to school.

The classical learning revived by the Renaissance, emphasizing learning for its own sake, had little appeal for Luther. His antihumanistic attitude threatened a break between the Reformation and the spirit of the Renaissance. The situation was saved by Luther's friend Philipp Melanchthon, who was a devoted scholar as well as a reformer. Melanchthon became a prime mover in the establishment of the modern German gymnasium. By publishing Greek and Latin grammars and other school books, as well as advising in the appointment of teachers, he contributed enormously to the success of these schools.

The educational progress represented by the Renaissance and the Reformation began to be undermined in the seventeenth century by a new scientific spirit. The radicals were no longer willing to accept the writings of the Greeks as the ultimate source of wisdom. Their point of view was expressed by Francis Bacon's *Novum Organum* (1620), in which it was maintained that truth is to be found in living rather than in books, that all ideas not derived from firsthand experience are of doubtful validity, and that words themselves may be used to conceal truth.

Further impetus to the movement away from the strictly classical tradition was provided by the accomplishments in scientific research led by such brilliant figures as Galileo, Kepler, Harvey, Descartes, Pascal, Boyle, Newton, and Leibniz. "Nature" and "reason" became key words in the era of Enlightenment, which ensued in the eighteenth century.

From an educational viewpoint, the intellectual ferment came to a head in the writings of Jean Jacques Rousseau, and most specifically in his book *Emile* (1762), which created widespread sentiment in Western Europe for a kind of romantic naturalism in education. The character Emile in Rousseau's novel is an orphan. He is removed from society altogether and his tutor for twenty-five years is his perpetual companion. Books are banned. Emile does not learn to read or write until he is twelve. Things or objects are his teachers and he discovers science rather than learning it. Thus in natural fashion the boy's physical, intellectual, and moral development are promoted until he is ready to take his place in society. According to Rousseau, all current educational practices were erroneous and should be rejected, because they failed to produce the morally noble individuals required by a free society. Rousseau opposed discipline, formal training, and restriction in general, holding that since the child is born morally good, the principal aim of education should be to prevent civilization from corrupting him. The child's only discipline should be natural punishment and his natural tendencies should be allowed free development.

Despite its follies and contradictions, *Emile* was an epoch-making book. It drew widespread attention to the subject of education and for the first time caused its readers to examine the problem from the child's point of view. In Rousseau's opinion, only the upper classes needed education, but his *Emile* inspired others, including Pestalozzi, to extend its concepts to the whole of humanity.

Common education was therefore in the air in the latter half of the eighteenth century and behind it was a new motive, philanthropy, the love of man. In Switzerland, a country closely associated with Rousseau, the improvement of education was a leading feature of an active social reform program. Unfortunately, the Swiss peasantry, whose condition was little removed from serfdom, lacked political influence, and progress was inevitably slow. Some members of the privileged classes attempted to ameliorate the lot of their dependents, and practical school reforms were introduced in such towns as Zurich, but because of the nature of the government—a loose confederation of eighteen tiny sovereign and twenty-seven semi-independent states—the establishment of any national system of education was impractical. Not until the 1798 revolution, supported by French bayonets, when the confederacy was broken up, was there any very discernible progress toward the reform of popular education.

We are informed by a number of contemporary accounts of the

oppressive conditions prevailing in the schools. In Canton Zurich there were some 350 country schools of which fewer than one hundred had buildings of their own. Their conditions were described by one writer of the time:

"As one opens the door, an oppressive damp strikes one. Packed in a dark corner sit our country's greatest treasure—its youth; they are compelled to breathe the hot air reeking with thick foul mist. The windows are never cleaned, the room is never aired. The children are so closely heaped together that it is impossible to get out without climbing over the seats and tables."[1]

A similar description of the ordinary Swiss school commonly existing when Pestalozzi was a child comes from another spectator:

The instruction was generally given in the schoolmaster's only living room, while his family were carrying on their household avocations. In places where there were schoolrooms, they were never large enough to provide sufficient space for all the children to sit down. The rooms were low and dark, and when the door was opened the oppressive fumes of a hot and vitiated atmosphere met the visitor; closely crammed together sat the children, to the ruin of their health, breathing in the foul and heated vapours. The stoves, too, were generally overheated, and the closed windows were darkened by the steam from the breath of so many human beings . . . . The noise was deafening; the schoolmaster had little authority over his pupils; there was no fixed age at which children were either sent or withdrawn; parents would frequently send them at four or five, and take them away as soon as they could earn any money, generally in their eighth or ninth year. The instruction was bad and irregular.[2]

In the practice of teaching, pupils memorized words, to be understood later, if ever, and teachers flogged unmercifully. The common result was that children were frustrated in spirit, confused in mind, and developed an active hatred of teacher and school. The situation was reminiscent of Shakespeare's reference to the schoolboy "creeping like snail unwillingly to school." The cruel treatment of the young was encouraged by the prevailing doctrine of "total depravity," according to which pupils were judged to be innately bad and averse to learning, a condition that could only be remedied by liberal application of the rod.

Most Swiss schools of the period were in private homes. A note left by one master remarks, "I keep school in my own house, and have only one room for both my household and the school. I receive no rent and no allowance for school furniture."[3] In a majority of villages the school was kept by a cobbler or a tailor, poorly paid and nearly always ignorant. His work was purely mechanical, he was rigidly conservative in religion and all other matters, and he adamantly refused to accept innovations.

The art of keeping school in Pestalozzi's youth was accordingly at a primitive stage. The children's duty was to learn and the schoolmaster's duty was to hear their lessons. Class teaching was unheard of in the village school. The children learned to read, and to say by heart the church catechism, selected portions of the Bible, and many prayers. Writing was usually taught only when parents wished it and the elements of arithmetic were regarded by many schoolmasters as a luxury. Method in teaching was totally lacking.

Pestalozzi's whole life may be regarded as a protest against the schools of his time. In *How Gertrude Teaches Her Children* he deplores the crippling of a child's mind caused when natural powers are deadened by poor home environment and excessive school discipline. The sad situation is described thus by Pestalozzi:

We leave children, up to their fifth year, in the full enjoyment of nature; we let every impression of nature work upon them; they feel their power; they already know full well the joy of unrestrained liberty and all its charms. The free natural bent which the sensuous happy wild thing takes in his development, has in them already taken its most decided direction. And after they have enjoyed this happiness of sensuous life for five whole years, we make all nature around them vanish from before their eyes; tyrannically stop the delightful course of their unrestrained freedom, pen them up like sheep, whole flocks huddled together, in stinking rooms; pitilessly chain them for hours, days, weeks, months, years, to the contemplation of unattractive and monotonous letters and, (contrasted with their former condition), to a maddening course of life.[4]

In another work, *Christopher and Alice*, Pestalozzi expresses his righteous indignation toward the schoolmaster's fondness for discipline, drill, and mechanical methods, all of which, he asserts, thwart the natural free development of tender minds:

The schoolmaster seems as if he were made on purpose to shut up

children's mouths and hearts, and to bury their good understanding ever
so deep under ground. That is the reason why healthy and cheerful children, whose hearts are full of joy and gladness, hardly ever like school.
Those that show best at school are the children of whining hypocrites, or
of conceited parish officers; stupid dunces, who have no pleasure with
other children; these are the bright ornaments of schoolrooms, who hold
up their heads among the other children like the wooden king in the
ninepins among his eight fellows. But if there is a boy who has too much
good sense to keep his eyes, for hours together, fixed upon a dozen letters which he hates; or a merry girl, who, while the schoolmaster dis-
courses of spiritual life, plays with her little hands all manner of temporal
fun under the desk; the schoolmaster, in his wisdom, settles that these
are goats who care not for their everlasting salvation.[5]

Various contemporary accounts bring out the heavily religious
character of instruction in the schools, a teaching method against
which Pestalozzi reacted violently. According to one such report,
the first school period each day was devoted to reading the Bible.
The children began where they had stopped the previous day
until they had "finished" the Bible. Immediately thereafter, they
started over again with Genesis and continued through Revela-
tion. Thus they read aloud the Old Testament, the New Testament, and the Apocrypha, with not a single word omitted, in a
period of about eight months. No effort was made by the schoolmaster to clarify or to explain obscure passages; at most he corrected a word which had been mispronounced. The contents
were mainly incomprehensible to the children and little explana-
tion was paid to their meaning.

Pestalozzi's scathing criticisms of the schools of his time concerned more fundamental wrongs than the physical mistreatment
of pupils. In his eyes, the prevailing teaching methods were almost completely irrelevant to the needs of society. He accused
the whole system, both in content and methods, of having become hopelessly bound by routine and tradition. Classroom
teaching had become so rigid that it did not take into consideration either the ability of the child to learn or the purpose of his
learning. In effect, the schools appeared to be organized to de-
stroy originality and imagination.

As summed up by Gerald Lee Gutek, in his *Pestalozzi and
Education*, "Pestalozzi's major attack on the verbalism and
bookishness of the traditional school was that it: (1) ignored and

weakened sense impression; (2) failed to teach essentials; (3) stressed the isolated teaching of special things; (4) produced letter men, artificially minded logicians; (5) separated theory and action."[6] By failing to utilize sense impression, the schools were neglecting the natural basis for all learning. The traditional learning process relied entirely upon the printed page instead of direct experience, which meant that students memorized printed words without understanding their significance. Further, Pestalozzi deplored the distinction between theory and action, or the separation of thinking and doing, characteristic of traditional education. Artificial or theoretical knowledge was useless unless applied practically.

It was in times like these that Heinrich Pestalozzi came upon the scene, filled with broad humanitarian impulses and the romanticism of Rousseau. Pestalozzi himself testified as to Rousseau's influence upon his career:

The moment Rousseau's *Emile* appeared, my visionary and highly speculative mind was enthusiastically seized by this visionary and highly speculative book. I compared the education which I enjoyed in the corner of my mother's parlour, and also in the school which I frequented, with what Rousseau demanded for the education of his Emilius. The home as well as the public education of the whole world, and of all ranks of society, appeared to me altogether as a crippled thing, which was to find a universal remedy for its present pitiful condition in Rousseau's lofty ideas. The ideal system of liberty, also, to which Rousseau imparted fresh animation, increased in me the visionary desire for a more extended sphere of activity, in which I might promote the welfare and happiness of the people.[7]

How much reform was urgently needed by the elementary schools of Switzerland, and indeed of all Europe, may be judged by the descriptions of eyewitnesses and participants quoted above. Heinrich Pestalozzi proved to be the right man at the right time to lead the campaign for major changes. From him more than any other individual came the spirit that inspired the great educational reforms of the nineteenth and twentieth centuries.

CHAPTER 2

The Early Years

I N the year 1555, a group of 117 Italian Protestant refugees fled from Locarno, now the capital of Italian-speaking Switzerland, to Zurich, to escape the oppression of the Counter-Reformation. At the time Zurich was one of the three most important Swiss centers of reformed Christendom. Among the refugees was Heinrich Pestalozzi's ancestor.

Heinrich Pestalozzi was born in Zurich on January 12, 1746, the son of a surgeon and oculist of some standing in the community. The father died at the age of thirty-three, when Heinrich was barely five years old, leaving a wife and three children in straitened circumstances. In order to meet the needs of the family with her extremely meager means, the mother had to practice the strictest economy and even endure privations. According to Pestalozzi's own account, "My mother sacrificed herself with the most utter self-devotion to the bringing up of her three children, depriving herself of everything which at her age and in her surroundings could have had attractions for her."[1] The mother was impractical and dreamy and had a strong sense of honor; she was determined to preserve her family's social rank. Contributions to worthy causes were made even when there was no money for new shoes or clothes. In all her domestic trials and troubles, the mother was tremendously aided by a faithful servant, Barbara Schmid, nicknamed "Babeli," who had promised the dying father never to abandon those whom he left behind.

The maid Babeli appears to have ruled the household with a firm hand. Money available for food had to be stretched to the limit, leading Pestalozzi to comment: "The trouble our Babeli took to perform impossibilities in this respect is almost incredible. In order to buy a basket of vegetables or fruit a few kreuzers cheaper, she would go back three or four times to the market and watch for the moment when the market-women wanted to go home." Babeli would often keep the children indoors when they wished to go out, saying to them, "Why will you needlessly wear out your shoes and clothes? See how much your mother denies herself in order to be able to give you an education; how for weeks and months she never goes out anywhere, but saves every farthing for your schooling." The three children always had "very grand Sunday clothes," but to preserve them had to change as soon as they came home.[2]

Though the tender, affectionate, and self-sacrificing mother and the loyal, sturdy maid dedicated themselves entirely to the welfare of the children, such rearing had serious drawbacks for Heinrich. He was weak and delicate from birth, a shy, awkward boy with an emotional temperament, imaginative, absent-minded, inattentive, and careless. His environment did nothing to build up his physical strength, since he was deprived of the company of other boys and did not participate in their active games. Pestalozzi attributed his own oversensitive, even unstable, nature to the lack of a father's firm guiding hand, though he was always deeply devoted to his mother and Babeli. The effects of the complete absence of masculine influence and physical training during his early years were described by Pestalozzi as follows:

Since the age of six, my surroundings offered nothing by way of manly training so urgently necessary for a boy of my age. I grew up in the care of the best of mothers as a spoiled child. Year in and year out, I was tied to my mother's apron strings. In a word, I lacked all the means and stimulation for developing the abilities, the experiences, and the ways of thinking befitting a man. The vigorous training which my nature with its peculiar disposition needed most was most deficient. . . . I was guarded like a sheep that was not allowed to leave the barn. I never contacted boys of my age on the street. I knew none of their games, their exercises, their secrets; naturally, I was awkward in their midst and the object of their ridicule.[3]

To the environmental restraints which kept him shut up at home may be ascribed Pestalozzi's early interest in intellectual activities. Most of his time was spent reading and listening to stories, with whose various heroes he often identified himself. Roger de Guimps, an early biographer, writes, "The boy, puny from his birth, always indoors, brought up entirely by women, deprived of a father's influence, of all contacts with boys of his age, remained all his life small and weak, shy and awkward, changeable and impressionable."[4]

Further psychological insights are offered by a later writer, Gustav E. Mueller, who concluded that the woman's regime by which Pestalozzi was surrounded "almost fatally reinforced his introvert and dreamy tendencies." Mueller continued: "He developed a self-pity which subsequently grew into a pity for all who are socially disinherited; in his Franciscan love of the poor, of orphans, beggars and the disabled, and in his zeal to improve their lot, is a personal quest to redeem his own unfortunate boyhood. And in his ideal to be a father to all children there is a bid to make good for his own lack of fatherly guidance."[5]

Pestalozzi was not, however, entirely lacking in masculine companionship. His summer vacations were frequently spent with his grandfather, Andrew Pestalozzi, pastor at Höngg, a village near Zurich. The grandfather not only served as pastor, but concerned himself with the education of the village children and cared for the welfare of all his parishioners. Through visits with the grandfather to the poor, sick, and distressed of the parish, young Pestalozzi became acquainted at first hand with the deprivations and suffering of the peasants. Filled with compassion for these unfortunate people and influenced also by his grandfather's social concern, Pestalozzi resolved at an early age to work for betterment of the lot of the masses. The grandfather's educational activities, in particular, impressed his young grandson, who in later years wrote: "His school, in spite of its defects from point of method, was a living bond between the moral life and the domestic education of the people, and this combined education influenced effectively and forcefully the practice of attention, obedience, industry, and effort and thus laid the basic foundations of education."[6]

Pestalozzi's admiration for his grandfather's accomplishments at first led him to choose the ministry for a career, seeing in that profession opportunities to help the poor and oppressed. The failure of his initial attempt to deliver a sermon, however, caused him to abandon the ambition to become a churchman.

Pestalozzi failed to shine at school. His education began in an elementary school, a so-called day school, and from there he moved to the grammar school, which he attended for three years.

He was always the butt for his schoolfellows' practical jokes, and he did not, for the most part, please his teachers, who saw little promise in a pupil who could not spell correctly, write legibly, or do sums in arithmetic. Social adjustment to other students was painful. According to Pestalozzi, "The boys in school sent me wherever they did not want to go and I did whatever they wanted me to do. Even at the time of the great earthquake when professors and pupils ran pell-mell down the stairs and none wanted to go back to the classroom, I went up and brought their caps and books down to them."[7]

Matters improved somewhat when, in 1754, Pestalozzi entered a seven-year preparatory school in Grossmünster, the Collegium Humanitatis, where he studied until 1757. For the final stage of his formal education, young Heinrich attended a higher second-ary school, the Collegium Carolinum in Fraumünster, an institu-tion that dated its origin back to Charlemagne in the eighth cen-tury. Both schools provided an environment well suited to Pestalozzi's nature. The curriculum in each was classical: Latin, Greek, and Hebrew languages, rhetoric and logic, followed by philology and philosophy.

While attending the Collegium Carolinum, Pestalozzi had the good fortune to come under the influence of several lively and inspiring teachers, foremost among whom were Johann Jacob Bodmer, professor of history, especially Swiss history, and Johann Jacob Breitinger, professor of Greek and Hebrew, whose impact on the development of German literature was profound.

The progressive ideas of some of the Carolinum faculty were not limited to literary matters, but extended into the field of poli-tics. In 1762 Bodmer established a political league known as the Helvetian Society, the members of which called themselves "Pa-triots," as they agitated for widespread political and social reforms. Bodmer, as a teacher of history and politics, was primarily in-terested in the history and social conditions of his own country. Many of the young men of Zurich, including Pestalozzi, joined the new society and resolved to dedicate themselves to lives of heroic self-sacrifice. Looking back on the movement some years later, Pestalozzi approved of the idealism and enthusiasm of the group, while concluding that its aims had been impractical. The weekly meetings of the Helvetian Society were devoted chiefly to debates on history, politics, ethics, and pedagogy, featuring political ideas emanating from Rousseau's *Social Contract* and *Emile*. A weekly journal, *Erinnerer*, founded in 1765, was the Society's literary organ, and Pestalozzi was one of its chief contributors. In articles propagating the members' views on moral reform, fearless attacks were made on "public abuses, dishonest and tyrannical officials, worthless ministers, and any person or practice which seemed to them to stand in need of reform."[8]

The meetings and publications of the Helvetian Society soon came under suspicion by the conservative authorities, who resented charges against them of abuses of power. Several cases of official corruption brought to light by the young members of the Society convinced the leading men of the town that attempts were being made to subvert existing institutions. Pestalozzi's future was directly affected. The author of a lampoon directed against the authorities, a young theologian, had escaped to avoid arrest for publication of a political article, and Pestalozzi was accused of helping him to flee. Though his guilt was unproved, he spent several days in prison and the costs of the action were assessed against him. Thenceforth Pestalozzi was regarded as a radical and dangerous demagogue by the magistrates. As a result, he was forced to forego plans for the legal career he had been contemplating.

After a serious illness, following these events, Pestalozzi was advised by his doctor to give up study for a time and to recuperate in the country. Already indoctrinated by Rousseau's teachings on the desirability of returning to a life of natural simplicity, agriculture appeared to him to be an ideal occupation. Rousseau had pictured the condition of the tiller of the soil as the happiest of all. "In the country of slavery," he declared, "one should be an artisan; in the country of liberty, one should become a farmer. A farmer can lead a peaceful life at home and cultivate the tender sentiments of the heart."[9]

The passion for nature had previously seized many young men under the influence of the Physiocrat Movement. Bodmer wrote, "It is astonishing how several of our best students have taken it into their heads to become farmers. They have already begun their apprenticeship by helping peasants reap, in order to see if they could endure heat, perspiration, rain."[10]

Upon the recommendation of one of his Carolinum professors, Johann Caspar Lavater, Pestalozzi decided to study agriculture under the direction of Johann Rudolf Tschiffeli, who was operating an experimental farm in the canton of Berne for training in modern farming methods. Tschiffeli was a gentleman farmer who specialized in the cultivation of clover for stock feeding, of madder for the red dye in the newly developed cotton industry, and of potatoes, which had only recently been introduced into Switzerland. His agricultural success had attracted wide attention, for he had converted a large tract of apparently worthless land into a number of valuable farms.

In September, 1767, Pestalozzi arrived at Tschiffeli's estate to remain for a year. His enthusiasm was boundless, as he writes, "Here I am and my happiness exceeds all expectation. Tschiffeli is the best of fathers, the greatest of farmers. I am going to learn farming in all its branches, and shall certainly become independent of the whole world. . . .I have now a lucrative career. Tschiffeli is really growing rich with his farm. I am learning the business thoroughly, and am sure I shall be able to set up for myself."[11]

Pestalozzi believed that he could emulate Tschiffeli's successful agricultural venture. What he did not realize and failed to learn until too late to modify his own plans was that the experimental farm was not economically self-sustaining. Actually, Tschiffeli had little business sense and would have been in serious financial difficulties had he not won first prize in a state lottery. The farm was largely supported from Tschiffeli's private income.

In any event, the idealistic and enthusiastic Pestalozzi had dreams of improving Swiss agricultural production, whereby the people could live in greater economic independence. He visualized the farm family, through a return to nature and to the soil, as becoming the moral center of Swiss life. With a small legacy from his father and some capital advanced by a banker in Zurich, Pestalozzi bought about a hundred acres of land near Birrfeld and began to cultivate vegetables and madder. The estate was named Neuhof, or New Farm. From the beginning, the enterprise was in difficulties. Pestalozzi was unbusinesslike in the extreme, as he was in virtually every venture to which he ever set his hand. He had been cheated in the purchase of the land by an unscrupulous agent. Further, the land was poor in quality and would require time, energy, and money to become productive. The banker who had provided financial support became alarmed about the safety of his investment and withdrew the promised loan. In addition, Pestalozzi found himself involved in legal quarrels with his neighbors, who ridiculed the gentleman farmer with his newfangled methods, and called him the "black pestilence." With ruin staring him in the face, Pestalozzi made an effort to recover his position by adding a wool-spinning business to the farm, a move that merely increased his problems and his debts, hastening a total financial collapse.

Always optimistic and hopeful, however, Pestalozzi built a house on his newly acquired, heavily mortgaged property. He had become engaged to Anna Schulthess, beautiful daughter of one of the richest and most respected families of Zurich. Their marriage took place in 1769, and the following year their only child, a son, Jean Jacques, named for Rousseau, was born. Through storm and stress over the next forty-five years Anna remained a faithful companion. The son was a weakling, subject to epileptic seizures, a grievous disappointment to his parents, and died at the age of thirty-one.

Despite the critical state of his finances, Pestalozzi decided to proceed with a plan that he had conceived to bring poor children into the Neuhof and to give them a simple education. It was the practice of the farmers of the neighborhood to take orphan apprentices from the parish authorities. If sufficiently overworked and underfed, the children proved profitable, but the consequences for the children themselves were disastrous. They grew up ignorant, illiterate, and degraded. Pestalozzi deplored this unhappy state of affairs and was further enraged by the new textile industry's exploitation of child labor. As he described the conditions around him:

I saw in a poor district the misery of those children who were hired out to the farmers by the municipalities; I saw how the oppressive harshness of self-interest, I might almost say, *condemned* nearly all these children in body and in soul; I saw how many, ailing and without courage and energy, could never grow up with those feelings of humanity, with those powers, which would be beneficial to themselves and to the fatherland.[12]

According to Pestalozzi's dream, Neuhof would become an industrial school, in which the children of the very poor might be trained physically, morally, and intellectually to live self-respecting lives. In summer the children were to work in the fields, in winter they were to spin and weave. Accompanying the handwork, the children would receive instruction in the elements of reading, writing, and arithmetic. The training received by the children, Pestalozzi insisted, must be tailored to fit the sort of life a poor child would lead when he left the institution. "The poor must be educated for poverty," stated Pestalozzi, "and this is the key test by which it can be discovered whether such an institution is really a good one. Education of the poor demands a deep and accurate knowledge of the real needs, limitations, and environment of poverty, and detailed knowledge of the probable situation in which they will spend their lives."[13]

During the winter of 1774-75, Pestalozzi and his wife began their work with about fifty poor, abandoned children, some of whom had been picked up in the streets and on the roads. Their ages ranged from six to sixteen; all were destitute and most were degraded and undisciplined. Many of the children had previously lived by begging and were tainted with vice. A vagabond life unfitted them for the strict routine and discipline necessary in a community such as Neuhof. Nevertheless, Pestalozzi clothed and fed them, treating them as though they were his own children. He was always with them, encouraging them to take part in all the work going on in the garden, on the farm, and in the house. The girls practiced domestic skills of cooking and sewing. Master spinners and weavers were employed to teach their arts to the boys and girls. All the children were given elementary instruction in reading, writing, and arithmetic, as well as in religion.

Any sign of gratitude on the part of parents or children for Pestalozzi's dedicated efforts on their behalf was largely lacking, at least at the outset. The parents often waited until the children had reached working age or had received new clothes and then persuaded them to run away from Neuhof and return home. But after several months some of the children began to respond, and Pestalozzi wrote, "It is an indescribable joy to see boys and girls, who had been wretched, growing and thriving, to see peace and satisfaction in their faces, to train their hands to work."[14]

From the beginning, the expenses of the Neuhof experiment far exceeded the profits. By the help of subscriptions and loans, there was a short period of apparent prosperity. Within a year, however, the existence of the institute was endangered from lack of funds. In 1776 Pestalozzi prepared and distributed an "Appeal to the friends and benefactors of humanity who may be willing to support an institution designed to provide education and work for poor children." He pointed out that gratifying success had been achieved with the children then attending his school. The response to the appeal was sufficiently generous to enable the institute to continue for a time. Contributions of a substantial and sustaining character, on the other hand, were another matter, despite the voiced support of leading citizens and a highly favorable report issued by a visiting committee representing the Bern Agricultural Society.

Pestalozzi's total ineptitude for practical administration was shown at Neuhof, as on later occasions. By 1779 he was forced to sell some of the land, and shortly thereafter it was determined that the institute was bankrupt and would be forced to close. The end came in 1780; the children had to be sent away, and Pestalozzi was left exhausted, penniless, and depressed. Without the assistance of friends and relatives, who saved the Neuhof house for them, the Pestalozzi family would have been left homeless. Even so, Pestalozzi was reduced to bitter poverty, largely forsaken by friends and relatives who had lost faith in his impractical dreams and schemes. He had also spent his wife's inheritance, and, to make matters worse, his wife, probably because of privation and worry, developed a serious illness from which she never made a complete recovery.

Pestalozzi himself did not accept the popular belief that the Neuhof experiment had been a total failure. As Michael Heafford comments in his excellent short biography, "his theories had been correct and the experiment gave him practical experience of organizing an institution and of teaching difficult and undisciplined children. Through this experience he had learnt that a successful education depended on providing a child with security and on giving him genuine affection. These were two principles to which Pestalozzi clung throughout his life."[15]

Some twenty years after the Neuhof institute had come to an end, Pestalozzi reviewed, with the aid of long-range perspective and hindsight, the aims and results of the venture:

I lived for years together in a circle of more than fifty pauper children; in poverty did I share my bread with them, and lived myself like a pauper, to try if I could teach paupers to live as men. The plan which I had formed for their education embraced agriculture, manufacture and commerce. In no one of the three departments did I possess any practical ability for the management of details, nor was my mind cast to keep up persevering attention to little things; and in an isolated position, with limited means, I was unable to procure such assistance as might have made up for my own deficiencies. In a short time I was surrounded with embarrassments and saw the great object of my wishes defeated. In the struggle, however, in which this attempt involved me, I had learned a vast deal of truth, and I was never more fully convinced of the importance of my views and plans than at the moment when they seemed to be for ever set at rest by a total failure.[16]

Pestalozzi recognized that if he had planned his project on a less ambitious scale, had established a sounder financial base in the beginning, and had started with a smaller number of children, ultimate success might have been conceivable. His tendency, as he noted, was "to try and climb to the top rung of the ladder leading to my aims, before I had set my foot firmly on the bottom rung."[17] On the other hand, a less ambitious and less idealistic man than Pestalozzi would have been unlikely to embark on such an undertaking in the first place. Even so, more than a hundred children had been rescued from ignorance, poverty, and degradation. Pestalozzi rightfully claimed: "I have proved that children after having lost health, strength and courage in a life of idleness and mendicity have, when once set to regular work, quickly recovered their health and spirits and grown rapidly."[18]

CHAPTER 3

Pestalozzi As Writer

FOLLOWING the collapse of the Neuhof experiment, Pestalozzi turned to a period of literary activity lasting for some eighteen years. His most significant literary contributions of an educational nature were produced between 1780 and 1798. Several earlier pieces of writing had included a diary, *How Father Pestalozzi Instructed His Three-and-a-Half Year Old Son* (1774), a detailed account of his experiments in applying Rousseau's ideas in the education of his child, and containing the germ of the author's theories of education according to nature,; therein Pestalozzi began to develop the principles of intuition and sense perception as educational bases. Shortly thereafter, Pestalozzi wrote three "Essays on the Education of the Children of the Poor," published between 1775 and 1778 in the periodical *Ephemerides,* edited by his friend Isaac Iselin.

Iselin remained Pestalozzi's firm supporter amid the latter's tribulations and encouraged him to write further contributions for his magazine. These writings enabled Pestalozzi to earn a living for his family. Among the first was a prize-winning essay on whether legislation against luxury is desirable and in the public interest; the conclusion was that luxury is not an evil in itself, because it may stimulate fine workmanship and bring a good income to artisans, but that it may become an evil if it takes the form of excessive ostentation and breeds greedy jealousy. More famous is a series of aphorisms by Pestalozzi, published anonymously in the *Ephemerides,* entitled *The Evening Hours of a Hermit* (1780), addressed to "the shepherds of the people and the wise of the earth." One of the first Pestalozzi biographers, Karl von Raumer, concluded that this work furnished "the program and key of Pestalozzi's pedagogical system, the plan of a gifted architect who is convinced of the value of the work which destiny has prevented him from carrying out."[1] Johannes Niederer, a later associate, notes that *The Evening Hours* contains the earliest outline statement of the whole range of Pestalozzian principles. Many of the 180 aphorisms relate to the author's views on improving the lives of his people through education. A characteristic example reads: "All the pure and beneficent powers of humanity are neither the product of art, nor the effects of chance. They exist virtually in the inmost nature of all men. Their development is a great need of humanity."[2]

Pestalozzi's only great popular success as a writer came with the publication in 1781 of the first volume of the four-volume work *Leonard and Gertrude*, "a novel of the people." Concerning the creation of the work, the author wrote, "The history of *Leonard and Gertrude* flowed from my pen, I know not how, and developed itself of its own accord, without my having the slightest plan in my head, and even without my thinking of one. In a few weeks, the book stood there, without my knowing exactly how I had done it."[3]

The scene of *Leonard and Gertrude* is the village of Bonnal. In the simple story, Pestalozzi pictures the far-reaching effects of a corrupt official. The lord of the village is Arner, who has turned over its management to his unprincipled steward Hummel. Every household in the small community suffers from the malicious influence of the man who is the village innkeeper and the official representative of the landowner. The people are for the most part sunk in degraded and depraved poverty. Among the residents are Gertrude, the heroine of the romance, a model wife and mother, and her husband, Leonard. Leonard is a man of weak character, easily led into wrong behavior, and he has fallen into the power of the unscrupulous tavern-keeper through borrowing money from him. To rescue her husband from the clutches of the steward, Gertrude goes to the castle to see Arner. The result of her visit is that Leonard is commissioned to build a church. Arner, the new squire, is anxious to do his duty by his people, and he initiates reforms that lead finally to the dismissal of the arch offender. Gertrude's household is described in simple, convincing pictures, setting forth her talks with her children, their eager response and willing help in the work of the home, their little acts of self-sacrifice toward each other and their neighbors. There emerges Pestalozzi's lifelong conviction that family life is the most potent of all forces for education and that the mother is the greatest teacher.

In the second and third parts of *Leonard and Gertrude* the need for educational reform comes to the fore. A spinner named Cotton Meyer suggests to Arner that "after all we can do very little with the people unless the next generation is to have a different training from that our schools furnish. Our schools ought really to stand in the closest connection with the life of the home, instead of, as now, in strong contradiction to it."[4] The squire, his friend Glüphi, and the village clergyman are arriving at the conclusion that permanent reform must begin with the children. The parents are perhaps beyond redemption, and children reared entirely in vicious home surroundings cannot be saved from moral ruin. The proper education of the young is the sole means of reforming the village. Gertrude's heart-warming effectiveness in education in her own home wins the attention and admiration of the village authorities, and after investigating her methods they decide to set up a school, with Glüphi as the schoolmaster who would introduce into the school Gertrude's spirit and ways. Glüphi has to overcome strong opposition from the parents and the children themselves, but eventually his work is crowned with success and he is recognized as a power for good in the community. Bonnal becomes a model village and its example is widely emulated elsewhere.

Pestalozzi had a double purpose in writing *Leonard and Gertrude*: first, to propagate his concept of an ideal educational system, and second, to point out ways and means by which social and economic reform could be brought about. He exposes the evils imposed on poor people by tyrannical and corrupt officials. It is further shown that a sufficient number of right-minded, honest, and dedicated citizens can stop corruption and establish clean government.

A leading Pestalozzi biographer, Henry Holman, comments that *Leonard and Gertrude* "has many passages of great eloquence, exquisite pathos, manly moralising, sparkling wit, dramatic intensity, riotous humor, fine character sketches, and charming incidents, in spite of its want of plot and great diffuseness."[5] These features account for the book's contemporary popularity, but in one important respect its reception was a disappointment to the author. The public bought and read it simply as an appealing and romantic novel, ignoring Pestalozzi's clarion call for society's reform. The second, third, and fourth parts of *Leonard and Gertrude* were met by a smaller audience than the first, because they were too much concerned with social, economic, and educational problems beyond the full comprehension of the average reader. Further, many readers considered the reform proposals set forth in the books to be impractical.

To make his views clearer, Pestalozzi undertook to write a "Second Book for the People," *Christopher and Elizabeth* (1782), a commentary on *Leonard and Gertrude*. Four characters—Christopher and his wife Elizabeth, their son Fritz, and a servant, Joost—discuss the meaning and application of every chapter of the earlier book. Christopher, a peasant, reads aloud to his family chapters from *Leonard and Gertrude*, after which their meaning is analyzed and the family's own observations and experiences of life are brought in. The actions of the fictitious characters, right and wrong, are compared with their own problems. Of *Christopher and Elizabeth*, one critic, Kate Silber, remarks, "Since it has no story . . . it lacks the pictorial qualities, the warmth of feeling, and the grim humour of its predecessor. It is tedious, and, as Pestalozzi himself admits, written in a dry, sententious style. It was not read either by ordinary or by cultivated people."[6] So was missed Pestalozzi's moral: that the proper education of the young is the foundation and cornerstone of true reform.

The following year Pestalozzi turned to another social problem: young women who killed their newborn infants because of the pressures of a society intolerant of illegitimate births. This piece, *On Legislation and Homicide*, discusses the mother's motives for such a desperate act and concludes that it is society rather than the mother who should be blamed. A greater degree of tolerance and forgiveness, Pestalozzi maintains, would make such violent acts less common.

During the years 1782-1783, Pestalozzi also published a paper of his own, the *Swiss News*. In the form of essays, dialogues, short moral tales, fables, and verse, Pestalozzi's views on education, politics, and social reform were presented to his readers. The essays deal with such subjects as the abuse of legal forms for defeating justice, one law for the rich and another for the poor, the hypocrisy of liberal sentiments among the privileged classes and their indifference to the real sufferings of the poor, domestic economy among the lower classes, the influence of different occupations on the character of the people, the state of the peasantry and of the manufacturing classes, the best interests of landed proprietors, parochial administration, the corruption of high life, the destructive effects of quackery and superstition, the moral improvement of criminals, the defects of charity schools, the duty of society to ensure every individual the means of gaining an honest living, and medical police. Dramatically written articles contrast the misery of the common people with the arrogance of the nobility. They deal with temptation and crime, and with such human vices as frivolity, greed, lust, and conceit. Pestalozzi's "Scene from the Mad-House," written after a visit to a lunatic asylum, is characterized by Silber as "a horribly impressive piece of psychological observation."[7] Not neglected in the *Swiss News* are thoughtful articles on questions of economics, legislation, and education. Another feature was a series of allegorical, Aesop-like tales related to the country's political and social conditions. An example is entitled "The Oak and the Grass":

One morning the grass said to the oak, under whose branches it grew: "I should get on much better in the open than under your shelter." "You are very ungrateful," replied the oak, "not to acknowledge the blessing, which you enjoy, of being protected from the frost in winter by the leaves from my autumn sheddings, with which I cover you."

But the grass answered, "You deprive me, with your branches, of my share of sun, dew, and rain; and with your roots my portion of nourishment from the ground; boast not therefore of the forced benevolence of your foliage, with which you foster your own growth rather than prevent my decay."[8]

Somewhat similar to these tales was Pestalozzi's *Illustrations for My ABC Book* (1787), intended to provide a number of short illustrative epilogues on morality, society, and education, to accompany *Leonard and Gertrude*. A second edition of the work was issued in 1795 under the title *Fables for My ABC*.

From a philosophical and theoretical standpoint, Pestalozzi's major writing achievement appeared in 1797, *Inquiry into the Course of Nature in the Development of the Human Race*. Therein he attempts to discover the basic motives for human behavior and to harmonize and reconcile education with the natural instincts and desires of man. Pestalozzi's prime objective was to gain a clear understanding of the aims of education. As he expressed his purpose, it was "essentially a means of becoming clear in my own mind about the development of my pet ideas and of reconciling my natural feelings with my conception of civil rights and of morality."[9] The work, which had been undertaken at the suggestion of the great German philosopher Johann Gottlieb Fichte, apparently made little or no impression on Pestalozzi's contemporaries. Pestalozzi comments:

For three years I took immense pains with my *Inquiry*, my chief object being to co-ordinate my favorite ideas, and bring my natural sentiments into harmony with my views on civil law and morality. But my work was but another proof of my incapacity. . . . And so I reaped no more than I had sown. My book had no more effect than my previous labors, nobody understood me, and there was not a man who did not give me to understand that he considered the whole work a jumble of nonsense. Only to-day even, a man of some distinction, and a friend, said to me: "Surely, Pestalozzi, you see now that in writing that book you did not really know what you meant."[10]

Impartial critics have disagreed with such disparaging remarks. One writer describes the work as Pestalozzi's "profoundest book, his philosophical *summa*, which he never surpassed."[11] Another describes the *Inquiries* as "without doubt the most searching of Pestalozzi's work."[12] A third rates the book as "significant in that it was one of the first attempts to produce a sociology of education."

The twenty-year period from 1780 to 1799 has been termed the years of inaction for Pestalozzi. During that long stretch of time, he had no opportunity to put his educational theories into concrete practice. He had to be content with expressing his ideas in writing. These were the unhappiest years of Pestalozzi's life, years when he was often filled with depression and despair, and suffering from serious privations. By no means, however, was it a period of futility or fruitless marking of time. His writings had, to a certain extent, made Pestalozzi famous. He visited Germany in 1792 and became acquainted with Goethe, Fichte, Wieland, Herder, and other prominent personalities. In the same year, he was declared a "Citizen of the French Republic," along with Jeremy Bentham, Tom Paine, William Wilberforce, Washington,

Madison, Friedrich Schiller, and Kozciusko. Too, he was offered attractive appointments in Austria, Tuscany, and Italian Switzerland, all of which he refused. In addition to writing books and numerous articles, Pestalozzi engaged in extensive correspondence with powerful political figures abroad, hoping to interest them in his ideas of educational and social reforms.

But despite the recognition and success Pestalozzi was gaining with his pen, he felt increasingly frustrated and isolated. It was not his ambition to become a writer. He did not enjoy writing and it was difficult for him, but he wrote in order to clarify his ideas and to relieve his mind. Writing was not a satisfactory alternative for the action in which he was so eager to take part. As Pestalozzi himself expressed the matter: "I was not brought up to be a writer. I feel at home when I have a child in my arms, or when a man who feels for humanity stands before me. And then I forget the poor truths fashioned by the pen. . . . For of everything which does not interest me as being indispensable to mankind I am unconcerned and the most ignorant of men."[13]

Though Pestalozzi insisted that "I want to be more than a mere writer," he continued to write until the end of his life, even after he had become deeply preoccupied with the real-life situations for which he had yearned. Three major works stand out from the later years: *How Gertrude Teaches Her Children* (1801), *Pestalozzi to His Age*, commonly called *Epochs* (1802-03), and his final work, *Swan Song* (1826).

How Gertrude Teaches Her Children, subtitled *An Attempt to Give Directions to Mothers How to Instruct Their Own Children*, is partly autobiographical in nature and a further exposition of the author's theories. The book consists of fourteen letters addressed to H. Gessner, Pestalozzi's publisher. There is no real "Gertrude" so far as is known, though a good deal of speculation exists on the point, and the "children" referred to are all children. In its influence, there is general agreement that the book has profoundly affected subsequent opinion and practice in education. This, the most famous and probably most important educational work produced by Pestalozzi, explains how his ideas on education had developed and how he had become convinced that his theories could be fitted into a single system. "For months," he states, "I had worked at the elementary stages of instruction and done everything to reduce them to the greatest simplicity; yet I did not know how they fitted together."[14]

The central point stressed by Pestalozzi in *How Gertrude Teaches* is that all truly human acitivty must be self-generated; therefore, the old educational methods of purely mechanical drill are psychologically unsound. Perception, developed by means of number, form, and language, is the fundamental source of all education. Also advocated is physical education, progressing from simple to complicated movements, and ethical or moral education based on the love between mother and child. "The aim of education," says Pestalozzi, "is not to turn out good tailors, bootmakers, tradesmen, or soldiers, but to turn out tailors, bootmakers, tradesmen, and soldiers who are in the highest meaning of the word, men. Consequently the aim of all education and instruction is and can be no other than the harmonious development of the powers and faculties of human nature."[15] Pestalozzi frequently compares the development of the mind to that of a tree. Nature, he points out, produces the largest tree from a tiny seed. Thus he arrives at an important practical principle: endeavor to make, in every action taken, gradual additions to knowledge; each new idea thus becomes an expansion of existing knowledge.

How Gertrude Teaches was another literary success, and Pestalozzi's contemporary fame as an educator rested principally upon the work. A steady stream of visitors came from all parts of Switzerland and Germany to observe at first hand the applications of Pestalozzi's method to an actual school situation.

Pestalozzi to His Age remained incomplete at the author's death. Its essential message is that man can restore himself to natural goodness through education. The history of the development of mankind is traced through five epochs, each leading to increasing corruption because of the self-interest of man's animal nature. The history of the race comes full circle from barbarism to barbarism. Ignorance and incompetence have brought about age-long debasement, which can only be corrected by a return to the original goodness of human nature. The first great teacher to enunciate these truths was Christ, who based the education of mankind on a belief in the dignity of man and the saving power of his better self.

Swan Song is a final statement of Pestalozzi's views on education, written at the age of eighty. He maintains that all aspects of education—the physical, the technical, the esthetic, the intellectual, the moral, and the religious—should be coordinated and harmonious. *Swan Song* is prefaced with a defense of Pestalozzi's career:

For half a century I have been seeking with unwearied activity to simplify the elementary instruction of the people and find for it such a path as Nature follows in developing and perfecting a man's various powers. During all this time, despite my many weaknesses, I have worked zealously for this one end. My want of skill has indeed often shown itself in the conception and execution of my enterprises, and has brought upon me endless sorrows; but till now I have borne them with unfailing patience, and without ever interrupting my serious efforts towards my end.[16]

The results of educational experiments extending over a long lifetime, Pestalozzi felt, could hardly be a matter of indifference to "the friends of humanity and education." He proposes, therefore, to provide "an account which will be as clear and precise as I can make it, and will tell not only of what has succeeded, but also of what has failed."[17] The *Swan Song* consists of two main parts: an account of Pestalozzi's ideas on elementary education, and the story of his life in terms of the success and failure of his varied undertakings.

Despite Pestalozzi's disclaimer that with him writing was a secondary interest, his works are voluminous. The first collected edition in German, 1819-26, ran to fifteen volumes. The most recent, sponsored by the Pestalozzianum and Zentralbibliothek of Zurich, 1927-64, is in twenty-one volumes. Innumerable editions of separate titles in scores of languages have appeared in print over the past two centuries.

CHAPTER 4

Pestalozzi As Schoolmaster

I   *Stans*

THE outbreak of the French Revolution in 1789 produced an unstable political situation in Switzerland. Radical doctrines promoted in France had crossed the border, penetrated the cantons, and divided Switzerland. An ancient structure that had survived for four centuries collapsed and fell under the revolutionary influence, carrying with it oligarchical governments, family and local privileges, and a host of rights, customs, and prejudices that had grown up, most of which had interfered with the liberty and equality of Swiss citizens. A new government, the Swiss Republic, one and indivisible, under a Directory of five members, was proclaimed, replacing the decentralized Swiss Confederation, which had been composed of some dozen cantons. Under the French army's compulsion, the upper classes were forced to renounce their many special privileges and submit to a democratic constitution.

Pestalozzi, in common with a majority of his countrymen, dreaded French intervention in Swiss home affairs, but by the beginning of 1798 such interference was an accomplished fact. Now reconciled to the situation, Pestalozzi became optimistic about the possibilities for progress, moral regeneration, and social reform under the new regime. Filled with patriotism, he offered his services to the Directory, preferably to be placed in charge of a new school in which he would have an opportunity to test his educational principles. Instead, he was appointed editor of a government newspaper, *The Helvetic People's Journal*, the aim of which was to improve the general education of the populace, win the goodwill of the people toward the government, and gain support for the new constitution. The attempt was unsuccessful, in part because the paper's content was too intellectual for a largely illiterate population, and in part because of the unpopularity of a government set up by a foreign power. After a few months, publication of the *Journal* was discontinued; Pestalozzi was editor for only six weeks.

Resistance to the national government was centered in the three cantons of Schwyz, Uri, and Unterwalden, with a long tradition of liberty, where the inhabitants were strongly attached to their ancient laws and customs, the Catholic faith, and the right to govern themselves by popular assemblies. The people felt nothing but hatred for the French Revolution and for the new directorate form of government for Switzerland. Accordingly, they refused to take an oath of allegiance to the Unitary Constitution.

A rebellion erupted in the mountain canton of Unterwalden, where a fanatical Catholic priest had promised the people that God would give them inviolable bodies and would send hosts of angels to support them in a holy war against the infidels. In September, 1798, a French army, passing through the canton of Nidwalden to attack the Austrians, met with armed resistance. The French retaliated ruthlessly with slaughter and devastation. After a fierce and bloody struggle, the French conquered the Alpine valley, killing hundreds of men and women who were fighting together, and burning down the villages, which were defended to the last house. Many children were left homeless and orphaned.

The federal government, shocked by the turn of events, at once began to take steps to repair the damage done in its name. A decision was made to open a poor-school in the capital village of Stans, Unterwalden, where homeless children could be brought together. Pestalozzi, who had rushed to the rescue and had already begun to gather terrified and starving orphans in the ruins of a monastery, was assigned the task of operating the institution. Here, at the age of fifty-three, Pestalozzi undertook the most arduous and heroic struggle of his life, but one offering a supreme test, for, as he stated, the "death or success of my aims." He added, "I was so anxious to be able to realize the great dream of my life that I would have started work in the highest Alps almost without fire and water, if only to have a chance to begin."[1] His wife and friends had implored him not to accept the appointment, because of age and health. Pestalozzi was adamant in his determination to go forward. To his wife he explained, "I am undertaking one of the greatest tasks of our time. If you have a husband who deserves all the contempt and rejection meted out to him, there is no hope for us; but if I have been misjudged and am worth what I myself believe, you will soon find me a comfort and support."[2]

The decree issued by the Directory for establishment of the orphan home and school contained the following provisions:

The immediate control of the poor-house at Stans is entrusted to citizen Pestalozzi. Children of both sexes, taken from among the poorest, and especially from the orphans in the Stans district, will be received in it and brought up gratuitously. Children will not be received before the age of five years; they will remain until they are fit to go into service, or to learn such a trade as could not be taught them in the establishment. The poor-house will be managed with all the care and economy that such an institution requires. The children will gradually be led to take part in all work necessary for the carrying on and support of the establishment. The time of the pupils will be divided between field-work, house-work, and study. An attempt will be made to develop in the pupils as much skill, and as many useful powers as the funds of the establishment will allow. So far as it is possible to do so without danger to the industrial results which are to be aimed at, a few lessons will be given during the normal labor. All the outbuildings of the women's convent at Stans are to be devoted to the purposes of the establishment, as well as a certain portion of the adjoining meadow-land. These buildings will at once be repaired and fitted up for the reception of eighty pupils. . . . For the founding of the asylum, the Minister of the Interior will, once for all, place a sum of two hundred and forty pounds at the disposal of the committee (Pestalozzi, Truttmann, sub-prefect of Arth, and the priest Businger of Stans).[3]

The difficulties confronting Pestalozzi at Stans appeared almost insuperable. The alterations and repairs in the convent building had begun at the wrong time of year, from the point of view of weather, and had gone slowly. The winter was early and severe and it was mid-January before the first children were admitted. Even then, the building was incomplete, unfurnished, and still occupied by bricklayers and carpenters. Pestalozzi opened the establishment with only one assistant, a housekeeper. As he described the situation, "Neither kitchen, rooms, nor beds were ready to receive the children. For the first few weeks I was shut up in a very small room; the weather was bad, and the alterations, which made a great dust and filled the corridors with rubbish, rendered the air very unhealthy. The want of beds compelled me at first to send some of the poor children home at night; and they came back next day covered with vermin."[4]

The children had other grievous afflictions, graphic details of which are related in an account left by Pestalozzi:

Most of them on their arrival were very degenerated specimens of humanity. Many of them had a sort of chronic skin-disease, which almost prevented their walking; or sores on their heads, or rags full of vermin; many were almost skeletons with haggard, careworn faces and foreheads wrinkled with distrust and dread; some brazen, accustomed to begging, hypocrisy, and all sorts of deceit; others broken by misfortune, patient, but suspicious, timid, and entirely devoid of affection. There were some spoilt children amongst them who had known the sweets of comfort; these were full of pretensions. They kept to themselves, regarding with disdain the little beggars who had become their comrades; tolerating this equality; and quite unable to adapt themselves to the ways of the house, which differed too much from their old habits.[5]

In some respects the most intractable and persistent of Pestalozzi's difficulties was the attitude of the community. The enterprise had to be carried on in the midst of political turmoil, which prevented the children having any sense of permanence or stability. The local population was outspokenly hostile, for two chief reasons: Pestalozzi was a Protestant in a Catholic area and he was regarded as an agent of the hated central government. Officials of the canton, as well as those in the Capuchin convent in whose outbuildings the poor-school was housed, were antagonistic to the scheme. There was also great opposition and much misunderstanding among parents. Pestalozzi was accused of underfeeding the children, of being too severe with them, and of using them solely for his own advantage. Children were encouraged to run away from the school after they had been fed and supplied with new clothes. As a Protestant, Pestalozzi was suspected of trying to convert the Catholic children. Well-educated citizens, accustomed to traditional educational methods, condemned him for any deviation from the pattern which they themselves had followed as children.

Undaunted by criticism and opposition, Pestalozzi dedicated himself completely to saving the youths placed in his care. Soon there were some eighty children of different ages and backgrounds housed in the school. With this heterogeneous group Pestalozzi lived in the closest contact. He writes:

From morning to evening I was virtually alone in their midst. Everything which benefited their bodies and souls came from my hand. Every piece of help, every form of succor in need which they received came directly from me. My hand lay in theirs; my eyes rested on theirs. My tears flowed with theirs and my smile accompanied theirs. They were outside the world, outside Stans, they were with me and I with them. Their soup was my soup, their drink my drink. I had nothing, no servants, no friends, no helpers with me, I had only them. If they were healthy, I stood in their midst, if they were ill I was at their side. In the evening I was the last to go to bed, in the morning I was the first to get up. I prayed with them and taught them in bed till they fell asleep.[6]

Despite all obstacles, the school was an immediate success, according to the testimony of various observers. Truttman, in a report to Minister of the Interior Rengger, dated February 11, 1799, noted that "the poor-house is doing well. Pestalozzi works night and day. It is astonishing to see how active this indefatigable man is, and how much progress his pupils have made in so short a time. They are now eager for instruction. In a few years the State will certainly be more than repaid for the sacrifices it is making for this useful institution." Another associate, the parish priest Businger, concurred: "Citizen Pestalozzi works incessantly for the progress of the establishment, and it is hardly credible how far he has been able to bring his work in so short a time."[7]

Pestalozzi was delighted to find that the educational theories about which he had written so extensively were highly successful in practice. The Stans experience was invaluable. He taught the children single-handedly, without help, a matter of choice, for he trusted no other teacher to understand fully and to effectuate his ideas. "I learnt the art of teaching many at once, and as I had no other means than that of repeating aloud to them, and making them repeat what I had said after me, the idea naturally occurred to me of making them draw, write, and work while they learnt. The confusion of the number of children repeating all at once conducted me to the necessity of making them repeat all together, in rhythm, and this speaking all together increased the impressiveness of what was taught."[8] Pestalozzi worked without any definite plan, without any apparent order, and without dividing the children into classes. He gave the children proof of his affection in everything he did and carefully cultivated every manifestation of their faculties, powers, and good impulses. The children's response was miraculous. As Pestalozzi recollected later, "I had children at Stans whose powers, not dulled by the weariness of unpsychological home and school discipline, developed very quickly. It was like another race. I saw the capacity of human nature, and its peculiarities, in full play—in many ways."[9] By creating a homelike atmosphere of love and emotional security, and being a father image to his household, Pestalozzi went far toward rehabilitating these victims of poverty and war. While some of the children remained obstinate and rebellious, a majority became cooperative and enthusiastic. According to Pestalozzi, "They felt through me they were getting further than other children; they realized the inward connection between my guidance and their future life."[10]

Since he had no helpers, Pestalozzi placed the unusually bright children between less capable ones to teach them what they knew, a learning device later more fully developed. While instructing the children in drawing, writing, and physical exercises, Pestalozzi encouraged them to cooperate with each other and to share their work. The theory of sense impression as the foundation of instruction had by now fully developed in Pestalozzi's mind. As he was convinced of the value of the natural environment for this purpose, the children were frequently taken on excursions to study natural history and the surrounding countryside. The Stans school possessed neither books nor school material; Pestalozzi rejected "artificial" means of teaching, preferring to make use of surrounding nature, daily events, and the children's own spontaneous activities.

May 24, 1799, was a memorable day for Pestalozzi and his pupils. On invitation, Pestalozzi took his whole establishment to Lucerne, where they were welcomed by the Executive Directory, the highest authority in Switzerland, and each child received a new silver coin. Unfortunately, the institution was near its end. About two weeks after the excursion to Lucerne, the school was closed. The French army retreating before the Austrians needed a hospital, they took over the convent for that purpose, and Pestalozzi and his children were dispossessed. Some of the children were returned to relatives, and homes in different families were found for the rest.

The effort Pestalozzi made at Stans was superhuman and proved too much for his health. The closing of the school was therefore a blessing in disguise, probably saving his life. He retired to the mountains to recuperate. While spending several weeks at the mountain resort of Gurnigel, he wrote a glowing account of his experiences at Stans. Though the school's existence was brief, the work Pestalozzi was able to accomplish there constitutes a landmark in the history of education. His orphan school at Stans has rightly been called "the cradle of the modern elementary school."[11]

In passing, it should be noted that Stans furnished a model for the "Pestalozzi Children's Village" in the foothills of the Alps in the small canton of Appenzell, established immediately after the Second World War to care for the hordes of homeless orphans wandering over Europe. Since opening its doors in 1946, the village has sheltered thousands of boys and girls six to eighteen years old. Similar children's villages have since been started in other countries around the world. These communities follow Pestalozzi's creed: give the children love and keep them occupied.

II *Burgdorf*

When Pestalozzi was sufficiently recovered from the exhausting experience at Stans, he was eager again to begin school work. His hopes of returning to Stans were frustrated by the opposition of Catholic parents. Pestalozzi therefore offered his services to the little town of Burgdorf, in the canton of Berne. At first, the request was refused, for reasons stated in Charles Monnard's *History of the Swiss Confederation*:

At that time the Burgdorf authorities would not have dared to entrust Pestalozzi with a primary school; this man, since so celebrated, would have had no chance whatever against even the most ordinary candidates. He had everything against him: thick, indistinct speech, bad writing, ignorance of drawing, scorn of grammatical learning. He had studied various branches of natural history, but without any particular attention to classification or terminology. He was conversant with the ordinary numerical operations, but he would have had difficulty to get through a really long sum in multiplication or division, and had probably never tried to work out a problem in geometry. For years this dreamer had read no books.[12]

To offset such weaknesses, Monnard notes that Pestalozzi possessed less obvious virtues: "he understood thoroughly what most masters were entirely ignorant of—the mind of man and the laws of its development, human affections, and the art of arousing and ennobling them. He seemed to have almost an intuitive insight into the development of human nature."[13]

No less a handicap than his lack of systematic knowledge of traditional school subjects was Pestalozzi's personal appearance. Johannes Ramsauer, a student of Pestalozzi's, describes him in these words:

Pestalozzi had a stocky, medium-sized body, more skinny than strong. At first glance he had an extremely ugly face which was very brown, full of small-pox scars and full of wrinkles. . . . As soon as he started to talk, his whole face was full of life and expression, and the gray, ugly eyes were full of spirit, love, and gentleness. His hair was very bristly and unruly, his clothes were neglected. He never wore a scarf or a bow which was fashionable at that time, except if a high visitor was expected, then he would throw it away as soon as he turned his back. A large brown coat without shape or pockets protected him against the weather. His stockings were usually hanging over his shoes and a heavy cap covered his head.[14]

Fortunately for his ambitions to resume a teaching career, Pestalozzi had friends in high places. In July, 1799, the Helvetian government assigned him as a teacher in the common vernacular school at Burgdorf, a small school in the lower town intended for the nonburgess or noncitizen class, attended by poor children whose parents were agricultural or industrial workers. The schools in the upper town were reserved for the children of the wealthy and the property owners. In his new position, Pestalozzi was to serve as a teaching assistant to the schoolmaster, Samuel Dysli, who was also a shoemaker. Dysli taught the children in his own house, and worked at his trade in the intervals of teaching, or perhaps concurrently. The school enrolled seventy-three pupils. The sole instruments for teaching and the entire curriculum were Siegfried's elements of instruction, the Heidelberg Catechism, the Psalms, and selected New Testament passages.

Pestalozzi proceeded to abandon this rigid program. Approximately one-half of the pupils were assigned to him, and these children had nothing to memorize, nothing to prepare or write, and no questions to answer. In place of individual recitations, Pestalozzi introduced simultaneous recitation, as at Stans, having the children repeat his words all together, while they drew on their slates. Neither readers nor copybooks were used and the catechism and Psalms were dropped from the daily lessons.

Samuel Dysli could not tolerate seeing a stranger teaching in his class, and, mistrustful and jealous, he concluded that Pestalozzi was attempting to supplant him. The new method was beyond his understanding and he was especially upset by Pestalozzi's neglect of the Heidelberg Catechism. Thus, Dysli began to spread rumors among the parents that the catechism was in danger and furthermore that Pestalozzi was unable to read, write, or do simple calculations. The alarmed parents declared that they would not permit the new master to experiment upon their children and demanded his dismissal. Once more Pestalozzi was unemployed.

Influential friends again intervened on Pestalozzi's behalf and procured an appointment for him in a dame school, actually an infants' school, where only children between four and eight, boys and girls, were admitted and taught reading and writing. In this small school of twenty-five pupils Pestalozzi was given a free hand. The atmosphere was thoroughly congenial to him. His genius and fatherly methods led to a triumphant success. "I sought by every means to simplify the elements of reading and arithmetic," Pestalozzi stated, "and by grouping them psychologically, enable the child to pass easily and surely from the first step to the second to the third, and so on. The pupils no longer drew letters on their slates, but lines, curves, angles, and squares."[15]

After Pestalozzi had been teaching in the school for eight months came the annual inspection by the Burgdorf school commission. A public letter from the commission to Pestalozzi warmly commended his work. The report, in part, reads:

The astonishing progress made by all your young pupils, in spite of their many differences in character and disposition, clearly shows that every child is good for something, when the master knows how to find out his talents and cultivate them in a truly psychological manner . . . the best of your pupils have already distinguished themselves by their good writing, drawing, and calculating. In all of them you have aroused and cultivated such a taste for history, natural history, geography, measuring, etc., that future teachers must find their task a far easier one if they only know how to turn this preparation to advantage.[16]

The commission went on to declare that the elements of learning could be acquired far more rapidly by following Pestalozzi's principles, reducing the time needed to be spent in the beginning stages, and giving the children a solid basis of useful information. In addition, the commission suggested that the method could be used effectively in the home by the mother or other intelligent members of the household in teaching children during the early years.

Doubtless because of the commission's favorable report, Pestalozzi was appointed master of the second boys' school at Burgdorf. This group of about sixty children ranged in age from six to sixteen. The curriculum included Bible history, geography, Swiss history, arithmetic, and writing. Here Pestalozzi resumed his experiments. As described by one of his pupils, Johannes Ramsauer, all teaching started from three elements: language, number, and form. There was no plan of studies and no order of lessons. Pestalozzi did not limit himself to any fixed time, often following the same subject for two or three hours at a time. The lessons lasted from eight to eleven in the morning and from two until four in the afternoon.

Pestalozzi was less successful in the higher class than he had been with the lower school. His method was designed for very young beginners and was too elementary for more advanced students. Ramsauer noted that "most of his pupils gave him a very great deal of trouble."[17] Pestalozzi's appearance and manners often compromised his authority in class. Within a short time, a pulmonary attack forced his withdrawal.

When he was well enough to continue work, the Helvetic government granted Pestalozzi the use of the castle at Burgdorf for a school. A Society of the Friends of Education, which had been formed on the initiative of Minister of Education Stapfer, for the purpose of promoting Pestalozzi's work, raised funds for preparing and furnishing the building. In the autumn of 1800, the school was opened, with the announced purpose of serving as a center for educational research, teacher training, and the preparation of instructional materials. The government allowed Pestalozzi to have the Burgdorf castle rent free, with wood for heating and gardening land; his salary was paid and support provided for his assistants. The publication of school books produced by Pestalozzi in the following years was subsidized and their copyrights protected.

Meanwhile, a number of poor children had been evacuated from the war-devastated canton of Appenzell in Eastern Switzerland and homes found for them in well-to-do Burgdorf families. Accompanying them was a young man, Hermann Krüsi, destined to play an important part in Pestalozzi's future affairs. Krüsi had continued to teach the children in a day school, also in the castle of Burgdorf, under the superintendence of the Secretary to the Helvetian Minister of Public Instruction, Fischer. After Fischer's sudden and unexpected death of typhus in Berne, Pestalozzi proposed a merger of the two schools, to which Krüsi readily agreed. Thus Pestalozzi acquired his first associate. The two men were in complete harmony in their educational philosophy. Moreover, Krüsi had to a high degree what was most lacking in Pestalozzi: the art of the practical schoolmaster. Too, he was willing to submit entirely to Pestalozzi's intellectual lead.

Also joining Pestalozzi as assistants at Burgdorf were several other able young men: Johannes Buss to teach drawing and singing, Johann Georg Tobler, to teach writing, Joseph Neef, and Johannes Niederer. The presence of this highly competent group helped to relieve Pestalozzi of his heavy burden of teaching.

The prosperity of the Burgdorf institute freed Pestalozzi to put into written form the principles of his method. These were embodied in his *How Gertrude Teaches Her Children*, published in 1801, a work intended to give the public a full account of his educational theories and practices. As noted earlier, the book spread Pestalozzi's fame abroad, expecially in German-speaking countries, and attracted numerous visitors to Burgdorf to see "the method" in application. Also emanating from the pens of Pestalozzi and his associates during the Burgdorf interlude were such textbooks as *Help for Teaching Spelling and Reading* (1801), and *Pestalozzi's Elementary Books* (1803), in parts: *The ABC of Intuition* or *Intuitive-Instruction in the Relations of Number, Intuitive-Instruction in the Relations of Dimensions,* and *The Mothers' Manual or Guide to Mothers in Teaching Their Children How to Observe and Think*, the last three meant to serve as teachers' handbooks on the elements of arithmetic, geometry, and language.

Visitors to the Burgdorf institute were particularly surprised by the children's rapid progress in drawing and in the elements of geometry. A distinguished Nuremberg merchant, who at first was prejudiced against Pestalozzi's ideas, wrote: "I was amazed when I saw these children treating the most complicated calculations of fractions as the simplest thing in the world. Problems which I myself could not solve without careful work on paper, they did easily in their heads, giving the correct answer in a few moments, and explaining the process with ease and readiness. They seemed to have no idea that they were doing anything extraordinary."[18]

Also impressed by the institute's accomplishments was a government commission sent to inspect the school in 1802. The commission's report commends Pestalozzi, "who had discovered the real and universal laws of all elementary teaching," and especially praises the moral and religious life of the establishment and the discipline, which, it points out, is entirely based upon affection.

Nevertheless, critics were not lacking. In her excellent biography of Pestalozzi, Kate Silber states: "The opposition to the Pestalozzian method had various explanations. In some instances it was simply due to envy of Pestalozzi's success and renown, in others the anxiety of religious and political orthodoxy to preserve traditional practices."[19] When all seemed to be going well at Burgdorf, political events again intervened. At the end of 1802, Napoleon announced his decision to revise the Swiss constitution. A national deputation was sent to Paris to interview the First Consul on behalf of the nation and to advise on the new constitution. Pestalozzi was elected a member. Prior to his departure he drew up a document outlining his own views of the responsibilities of government; its chief objects, he stated, should be to establish a suitable scheme of popular education, with an organized system of higher and professional schools based thereon, a sound judiciary, a good military system, and sound finance.

Pestalozzi had hoped to interview Napoleon while in Paris and to draw attention to his educational ideals, but Napoleon sent word that he was too busy to trouble about his ABC. The Paris mission proved fruitless, not only for Pestalozzi but for the entire Swiss delegation. Napoleon had made up his mind to dissolve the central government and to restore all administrative power to the cantons. The Act of Mediation signed by the Emperor early in 1803 was a disaster for the Burgdorf school. Pestalozzi's dreams of future support vanished when the unitary government ceased to exist. The new government in Berne, which took possession of the castle, had little sympathy for Pestalozzi, whom it considered a revolutionary and a radical. Notice was given to Pestalozzi to vacate the castle, on the pretext that it was needed as the residence of the prefect of the district. In June, 1804, Pestalozzi's connection with Burgdorf came to an end.

Pestalozzi again was not without powerful influence, however, and to save themselves in the eyes of their critics, the authorities offered him the unused rooms of an old monastery of Münchenbuchsee, about three miles from Berne, and within a mile of Emmanuel Fellenberg's agricultural and philanthropic institution at Hofwyl. Fellenberg, another pioneer in education, had much in common with Pestalozzi, as a consequence of which the two men agreed to combine their schools. On the surface, the plan seemed ideal: Pestalozzi was to be in charge of the educational phases and Fellenberg to manage the financial and administrative side, for which he was experienced and well fitted. The agreement proved unsatisfactory to Pestalozzi, however, because of Fellenberg's dominant personality and inclination to assume control of everything.

When Pestalozzi had been forced to leave Burgdorf, he had been offered the use of the castle at Yverdon, and some of his staff and students had transferred to that location. In October, 1804, after his final break with Fellenberg, Pestalozzi moved to Yverdon, where he was to spend the remainder of his educational career.

CHAPTER 5

Practical Applications

PESTALOZZI'S written expressions of his educational theories are not infrequently obscure and occasionally are inconsistent. An examination of the actual applications of his methods to specific subject fields, therefore, should be enlightening. Characteristic features appear in his views on the teaching of arithmetic, drawing and writing, language, geography, music, science, and physical education. As Hermann Krüsi, son of Pestalozzi's first associate, pointed out, however, there are also inconsistencies to be watched for in analyzing methodologies. For example, Pestalozzi has left no clear descriptions of his approaches to the teaching of some important fields of study, and his experiments and scattered exercises were often modified by his associates. Krüsi notes that "many of Pestalozzi's own experiments were obviously failures, and were abandoned as soon as tried. Subsequent investigation has shown that they were often antagonistic to the principles which they sought to embody. Even as modified by his associates and used in his Institution they were necessarily crude, and have since been greatly improved."[1] Insofar as patterns can be traced, an attempt will be made here to show the practical applications of Pestalozzi's theories in his various schools.

I *Arithmetic*

The most highly developed subject at Yverdon was mathematics. In Pestalozzi's view, arithmetic offers the most lucid areas of any subject—the aim of all instruction. As in the teaching of language and form, the teaching of numbers should be based upon sensory experience. Pestalozzi describes, in the introduction to his *ABC of Number Relations*, how mothers should endeavor to give numerical notions to their children. The mothers are advised to let their children count peas, leaves, pebbles, sticks, and other objects until the abstract idea of numbers is awakened in their minds. From the moment when the child begins to use his senses, Pestalozzi states, "I endeavor to make upon the child that firm impression of the relations of numbers, as such actual interchanges of more and less, as may be observed in objects discernible by the eye. The first tables of that work contain a series of objects intended to bring distinctly before the eyes of the children the ideas of one, two, three, etc., up to ten."[2]

The introductory lessons in arithmetic consisted of what Pestalozzi called the elements of number. In his *Letters on Early Education* (1819), he holds that the elements "should always be taught by submitting to the eye of the child certain objects representing the units. A child can conceive the idea of two balls, two roses, two books; but it cannot conceive the idea of 'two,' in the abstract. How would you make the child understand that two and two make four, unless you can show it to him first in reality?"[3] Proceeding in opposite fashion from the traditional method of the teaching of arithmetic, therefore, Pestalozzi did not set out to teach his pupils how to do sums but instead how to understand numbers. The assumption was that if his pupils understood numbers, they were able to do sums, easily and accurately. On the other hand, children who merely learn to do sums may never understand numbers. Pestalozzi's pupils were able to discover the ordinary rules of arithmetic from their study of the principles of numbers. Under the other system, the children learned the rules by memory and worked the sums unintelligently.

Pestalozzi began his number teaching by giving the students the conceptions of numbers from one to ten, first with the help of actual objects and later by lines and dots on tables. Not until the children had been thoroughly drilled in the counting of objects, such as peas and pebbles, did the classroom instruction proceed to figures, which were regarded as abbreviations of what had been learned through sense impressions. Abstract mathematical principles and tables to be memorized by students were shunned by Pestalozzi; on the contrary, he always began with concrete objects. After the child became proficient in the counting of real objects he was exposed to Pestalozzi's specially designed counting tables. According to Pestalozzi, "If, for instance, we learn merely by rote 'three and four make seven,' and then we build upon this 'seven,' as if we actually knew that three and four make seven, we deceive ourselves; we have not a real apprehension of seven, because we are not conscious of the physical fact, the actual sight of which can alone give truth and reality to the hollow sound."[4]

All through the teaching of numbers, Pestalozzi's aim was to develop distinct ideas through grouping (addition and multiplication), separating (subtraction and division), and comparing (ideas of more or less) the objects of perception.

Three arithmetical tables were used by Pestalozzi in teaching numbers: Table of Simple Unity, Table of Simple Fractions, and Table of Compound Fractions. In the Table of Simple Unity there were ten of each number on a line, e.g., ten ones, ten twos, ten threes, etc. The Table of Simple Fractions contained ten squares in each line and ten lines, the last line consisting of ten squares divided into tenths. The Table of Compound Fractions also had ten lines and ten squares in each. In the first line the unit was divided in halves, thirds, etc., to tenths; in the second line, halves were divided into their halves, thirds, etc., to tenths; and in the last line tenths were similarly divided. After the simple rules had been mastered, the student was taken to fractions, and finally his knowledge was applied to practical arithmetic—money, weights, measures, etc.

Training in real rather than abstract numbers, Pestalozzi maintained, enabled the child "to enter with the utmost facility upon the common abridged modes of calculating by figures. His mind is above confusion and trifling guesswork; his arithmetic is a rational process, not merely memory work, or mechanical routine; it is the result of a distinct and intuitive apprehension of number, and the source of perfectly clear ideas in the further pursuit of that number."[5]

The success of Pestalozzi's methods is attested by various visitors. In a letter to an English educator, J. P. Greaves, dated April 17, 1819, Pestalozzi described the "astonishment at the perfect ease and the quickness with which arithmetical problems, such as the visitors used to propose, were solved." This fact convinced Pestalozzi of the validity of his elementary method; he added that it "went a long way, at least with me, to make me hold fast the principle, that the infant mind should be acted upon by illustrations taken from reality, not by rules taken from abstraction; that we ought to teach by *things* more than by *words*." Further, children trained by the Pestalozzian scheme "were perfectly aware not only of what they were doing but also of the reason why. They were acquainted with the principle on which the solution depended; they were not merely following a formula by rote."[6]

Another advantage pointed out by Pestalozzi was that "children well versed in these illustrative elementary exercises afterwards displayed great skill in mental arithmetic. Without repairing to their slate or paper, without making any memorandum of figures, they not only performed operations with large numbers, but they arranged and solved questions which at first might have appeared involved, even had the assistance of memoranda or working out on paper been allowed."[7]

The idea of having boys of all social ranks and mental abilities learn algebra and geometry was opposed by Pestalozzi. Advanced mathematical knowledge is needed by few persons, in his judgment, and special training in that area should be confined to students of superior mental ability.

II *Geography*

Concreteness and sense perception also marked Pestalozzi's concepts of the teaching of geography. In his *Fundamental Principles of Method*, Pestalozzi outlines the scope of the material dealt with in this field:

Instruction in geography begins with a study of the earth and how nature has formed it (physical geography); then proceeds to boundaries which the inhabitants of the earth have settled in the course of time, and of the use they have made of the area within the boundaries (political geography); and to a consideration of the powers of the states and their sources of help and to their relative importance (statistics); and finally to mathematical geography; to the wonderful relations of our planetary system, and an appreciation for the wisdom and power of its Creator.[8]

Pestalozzi had doubts that geography was a suitable subject in the elementary curriculum. Apparently he resolved these doubts by the device of bringing geographical data as close to home for the students as possible. The beginnings of physical geography, for example, were taught by observing the different conditions of water, at rest or in motion, its form as dew, rain, vapor, steam, frost, hail, etc., and water's action on other natural objects. The children were taught to oberve the country around their own home, not from a map, but by walking expeditions. They were furnished with blank maps to be completed by actual observations.

Several accounts have survived, written by Pestalozzi's pupils, of his teaching methods for geography. One, by Louis Vulliemin, who became an eminent historian, is recorded in Guimps' biography of Pestalozzi. Vulliemin, who spent two years of his boyhood at Yverdon, from the age of eight to ten, wrote:

The first elements of geography were taught us from the land itself. We were taken to a narrow valley not far from Yverdon, where the river Buron runs. After taking a general view of the valley, we were made to examine the details, until we had obtained an exact and complete idea of it. We were then told to take some of the clay, which lay in beds on one side of the valley, and fill the baskets which we had brought for the purpose. On our return to the Castle, we took our places at the long table, and reproduced in relief the valley we had just studied, each one doing the part which had been allotted to him. In the course of the next few days more walks and more explorations, each day on higher ground, and each time with a further extension of our work. Only when our relief was finished were we shown the map, which by this means we did not see till we were in a condition to understand it.[9]

One of the warmest tributes to Pestalozzi as a teacher of geography came from Karl Ritter, an outstanding nineteenth-century geographer. Ritter attributes much of the success of his own career to Pestalozzi's influence, commenting that "Pestalozzi knew less geography than a child in one of our primary schools; yet it was from him that I gained my chief knowledge of this science, for it was in listening to him that I first conceived the idea of the natural method. It was he who opened the way to me and I take pleasure in attributing whatever value my work may possess entirely to him."[10]

Baron Roger De Guimps himself, from whom the foregoing Vulliemin and Ritter quotations are taken, was a pupil in Pestalozzi's school in Yverdon, and described the excursions into the country for the purpose of studying geography and natural history. Concerning his experiences he wrote:

These excursions into the Jura were a source of great delight to us. They were arranged to suit the ages of the different classes, and as soon as I was seven I began to take part in them. Our masters looked after us with almost motherly solicitude, making frequent halts to rest our little legs. . . . As soon as we got to the high mountain pastures under the pines, we lost our feeling of fatigue, and fell to playing games or collecting herbs or minerals. . . . On returning from one of these excursions, the pupils had to describe them, either orally or in writing, according to their ages. There was generally a great deal to say, as our attention was always carefully drawn to everything likely to prove instructive.[11]

Pestalozzi's major principle in teaching geography was to move from the near to the far. Not until they had become thoroughly familiar with their own locality were children introduced to broader areas. After exploring the immediate vicinity of the school, they moved out to study the neighborhood, the district, the canton, the country, and finally continents and oceans. The field trips were designed to examine the plant and animal life of the area as well as topography. Hermann Krüsi observed that the fundamental concept in Pestalozzi's method of geographical instruction was that 'the perception of a hill will lead to the comprehension of a mountain; of the windings of a brook, to the knowledge of an island, a peninsula, an isthmus, a bay, a cape, and a sea. With this sure basis of thorough home knowledge, the pupil prepared to comprehend the essential features of the countries which lie beyond the reach of his personal observations; for then he holds the key of all geographical knowledge."[12]

III   *Science*

The Pestalozzian nature study methods were closely analogous to those followed in geography teaching. Concrete perception was stressed. Even more than of most subjects, Pestalozzi believed that the true basis of scientific knowledge was sensory experience, and scientific education should be based on personal, first-hand observation. Field trips, walks through woods, and mountain climbing excursions were therefore integral features of science instruction in the Pestalozzian institutes. Trees, flowers, and birds were viewed, drawn, and discussed.

In his *Swan Song*, Pestalozzi states his belief that any child, no matter how limited in experience, is certain to become familiar with certain mammals, birds, fishes, insects, amphibians, and worms. Thus every child's natural environment has provided a foundation for scientific study. Pestalozzi argues further that if a child has observed in his mother's kitchen the phenomenon of the solubility of salt and sugar, and is familiar with the fact that it can be again recovered from a solution by crystallization and evaporation; if he is familiar with fermentation of wine and its turning sour and becoming vinegar; if he has seen the transformation of alabaster into plaster, marble into lime, and sand into glass, he has acquired elementary scientific principles and is prepared to build upon these known facts.

An understanding of Pestalozzi's methods can be gained by a statement addressed by him to fathers, in which he urges that "they should lead their children out into Nature and teach them on hilltops and valleys." Actually, nature will do the teaching: "Let the child realize that she is the real teacher and that you and your art have no other purpose than to walk quietly at her side. If a bird should sing or an insect should crawl on a leaf, stop your conversation immediately; the bird and insect are teaching him more and better. You may keep still."[13]

An early Pestalozzi biographer, Eduard Biber, assessed Pestalozzi's science teaching methods as follows:

Natural history and physical science were taught entirely without plan, though, in some instances, in a manner decidedly superior. The children were led to observe and to examine for themselves such objects and phenomena as were within reach; and, to enlarge the sphere of their knowledge, their teachers made excursions with them in different directions through the country . . . in a country so eminent for the abundance and variety of its natural productions, it was impossible that the pupils should not under the guidance of intelligent teachers, acquire rich stores of real information.[14]

Biber cited one serious objection to the method: "the students did not acquire a comprehensive view of the sciences." The teaching was largely of a demonstrative nature and essentially casual, as a consequence of which the children's knowledge, as Biber stated, "had a tendency afterwards to remain fragmentary."[15]

Physics and chemistry were also included by Pestalozzi in the curriculum of the school at Münchunbuchsee. In his *Report to Parents*, Pestalozzi commented on the program:

We are also trying at the same time to organise the teaching of experimental science. So far we have demonstrated to the boys the principal facts concerning Electricity and Magnetism and the behavior of certain gases. We are, in this connection, trying to establish a satisfactory course of instruction in the language of physical science. A local doctor gives weekly lessons in this direction to the older children with the aid of excellent apparatus in his possession.[16]

Pestalozzi's influence on science teaching, especially in England and America, was perhaps most evident in his object lessons. In the training of teachers and in textbooks on methods of teaching, object lessons received particular attention. An English Pestalozzian, Elizabeth Mayo, in her *Lessons on Objects*, for example, presented typical object lessons on numerous scientific subjects, and these served as models to many teachers.

IV *Music*

Pestalozzi is due credit for the practical introduction of music into the primary school curriculum, even as early as Neuhof. He believed firmly that music was an aid to moral education. Krüsi claimed that "of the science of music Pestalozzi knew nothing, and although he by no means undervalued it as an intellectual process, yet he regarded it chiefly in its softening and humanizing effects upon character and society."[17] In Pestalozzi's own words:

It is not proficiency in music which I consider most important. It is the marked and most beneficial influence which it has on the feelings, and which I have always thought to be very efficient in preparing and attuning us for the best impressions. The exquisite harmony of a superior performance, the studied elegance of the execution may give satisfaction to a connoiseur; but it is the simple music which speaks to the heart. The natural melodies, which have from time immemorial been resounding in our native valleys, are fraught with reminiscences of the brightest parts of our history, and of the most endearing scenes of domestic life. The effect of music in education is not alone to keep alive a national feeling; it goes much deeper. If cultivated in the right spirit, it strikes at the root of every bad or narrow feeling, of every ungenerous or mean propensity, of every emotion unworthy of humanity.[18]

Music teaching should begin, Pestalozzi believed, with the lullabies the mother sings to the child in the cradle and then gradually progress into national songs and hymns of praise. In a letter shortly before his death, dated February 18, 1827, Pestalozzi wrote: "Those schools or those families, in which music has retained the cheerful and chaste character which it is so important that it should preserve, have invariably displayed scenes of moral feeling, and consequently of happiness, which leave no doubt as to the intrinsic value of the art."[19] Pestalozzi cites Martin Luther as an authority who advocated simple, solemn, and impressive music as one of the most effective devices for arousing feelings of devotion.

At Burgdorf, Johann Christoph Buss was the teacher of music. According to another assistant, Johannes Ramsauer,

The thirty or forty children of both sexes in Pestalozzi's old school came from the town to the castle to take part in the singing. Buss made his pupils sing as they walked, two by two, holding each other's hand, up and down the big corridors of the castle. This was our greatest pleasure. . . . Indeed singing was one of our chief sources of enjoyment in the institute. We sang everywhere—out of doors, during our walks, and, in the evening, in the court of the castle; and this collective singing contributed, in no small degree, to the harmony and good feeling which prevailed among us.[20]

A similar account comes from Guimps, describing the mountain excursions from Yverdon: "We would sing gaily as we passed through the villages, where the peasants often gave us fruit. As soon as we got to the high mountain pastures . . . we often assembled at some good point of view to sing the wild, simple Alpine melodies our masters loved to teach us."[21]

The first application of Pestalozzi's principles to the teaching of music was made by his friend Hans Georg Nägeli, an eminent Swiss composer, and Michael T. Pfeiffer, who had spent two years with Pestalozzi at Burgdorf. Both men were doing much for the popularization of music in Switzerland, and Pestalozzi invited them to apply his general educational methods to the teaching of music, helping in that way to introduce it into the life of the people. The result of their efforts was the publication of a book, *The Teaching of Music on Pestalozzian Principles* (1810). The work begins with general preliminary training followed by more specialized courses, consisting of the singing of words, the relative time and word emphasis, the connection of music and poetry, and introduction to musical works.

In a report to parents and the public on the progress of the school at Yverdon, Pestalozzi outlined the nature of the music program in that institution. Instruction was limited, he noted, to vocal music, which included work in harmony, tempo, and the fundamentals of reading and composing music. Every Sunday morning the pupils sang as an organized group. Those interested in instrumental music could obtain lessons in piano, violin, flute, and clarinet in the city.

V *Drawing and Writing*

Great stress was placed by Pestalozzi on form, which he subdivided three ways: the art of measuring, the art of drawing, and the art of writing. "In endeavoring to teach writing," he remarks, "I found I must begin by teaching drawing; and when I took the latter in hand, I saw that the art of measuring was involved." He notes further that "a taste for drawing invariably manifests itself in the child without any assistance from art; while the task of learning to read and write is, on account of its difficulty, so disagreeable to children that it requires great art or great violence to overcome the aversion which they often evince."[22]

Pestalozzi concluded that "drawing ought to be a universal acquirement, because the talent for it is universally inherent."[23] He found that the attempt to draw is one of the earliest activities of the child, who is led to drawing through the eye and the hand. Because it is natural for children to want to imitate objects that they see, the power to imitate, to represent by drawing, should be recognized at a very early age. To stimulate this tendency, Pestalozzi advised that children should be given a variety of playthings to sharpen their observation and gain their interest. He adds:

In proposing, however, the art of Drawing as a general branch of education, it must not be forgotten that I consider it as a means of leading the child from vague perceptions to clear ideas. To accomplish this object, it must not be separated from the art of measuring. If the child be made to imitate objects before he has acquired a distinct idea of their proportions, his instruction in the art of Drawing will fail to produce upon his mental development that beneficial influence which alone renders it valuable.[24]

Early practice in drawing brings important advantages to the individual, in Pestalozzi's view. In his book *On Infants' Education*, he observes that "even in common life, a person who is in the habit of drawing, especially from nature, will easily perceive many details which are commonly overlooked, and form a much more correct impression, even of such objects as he does not stop to examine minutely, than one who has never been taught to look upon what he sees with an intention to reproduce a likeness of it. The attention to the exact shape of the whole, and the proportion of the parts, which is necessary for the taking of an adequate sketch, becomes a habit."[25]

In the same work, Pestalozzi recommends that children's drawing exercises be based upon natural objects instead of having the child copy another drawing. He goes on to point out that "the impression which the object itself gives, is so much more striking than its appearance in an imitation. It gives the child much more pleasure to be able to exercise his skill in attempting a likeness of what surrounds him, and of what he is interested in, than in laboring at a copy of what is but a copy itself, and has less of life or interest in its appearance."[26] Also, Pestalozzi maintained that perceptions of light, shade, and perspective can be gained solely by placing real objects before the children.

Pestalozzi theorized that the power of clear representation of all real objects depended upon the early development of the ability to draw lines, angles, rectangles, and curves. Before starting to draw an object, therefore, children should learn the simple elements of the laws of form and the art of measuring. For this purpose, Pestalozzi's assistant Johann Buss constructed an "alphabet of form," consisting of various lines of a figure drawn within a square—vertical, horizontal, and diagonal lines and arcs placed in the four principal points of direction, showing circles, semicircles, quarter-circles, and various ovals. The child was expected to learn the different kinds of lines and angles and the divisions of the square and circle before proceeding to draw figures using these lines. The opinion of various critics, however, is well represented by Pestalozzi's biographer, Henry Holman, who concluded that "the mechanism of the training became much too elaborate, and therefore hindered and obstructed the higher development."[27]

The art of writing, according to Pestalozzi, should be taught after measuring and drawing. Practice in drawing, he believed, made the formation of letters easier, because "writing is only a kind of linear drawing applied to arbitrary forms and must be subject to the general laws governing linear drawing."[28] A child is able to draw pictures at least two years before he develops enough skill to write well. The accuracy, precision, and perfection acquired in drawing is readily transferred to the formation of letters.

In *How Gertrude Teaches Her Children,* Pestalozzi proposes that writing should be taught in two stages: "The first when the child is to learn the formation and combination with the slate pencil merely; and the second when he is to practice his hand in the use of the pen." During the first stage the child used a writing book containing letters to be copied on a slate. He proceeded gradually from the simple forms of the letters to the complex and then to combinations of several letters. Not until the child had learned by practice to write the letters perfectly on a slate was he permitted to write the exercises with a pen. "In this manner," Pestalozzi comments, "the child learns to write with ease and perfection in the first course, and all that remains to be done in the second is to teach him the use of the pen. This is to be done by the same gradual process which was followed on the slate; the letters are to be drawn with the pen on the same enlarged scale which was adopted for the first attempt with the pencil, and to be diminished, gradually, to the usual size."[29]

VI *Language*

All elementary education, Pestalozzi claimed, was based on language, number, and form, the latter two of which have been discussed. For Pestalozzi, language was more than a means of communication:

Language . . . is indispensable to the development of our humanity. . . . To man language is given as a means of expressing his reflections, his feelings, his aims, his hopes, and his worries. Language is in itself . . . the essence of the mental consciousness the human race has of itself and of nature. Therefore as every *human* activity is inseparable from con-

sciousness and only through the latter reveals itself according to its nature as human, so is talking inseparable from all human learning and activity. Just as the child cannot become clearly conscious of his natural
observations and impressions without language, so will he not be able
to attain knowledge of the very first element of number and form.[30]

Before children are ready to learn to read, Pestalozzi held,
they must have learned to talk, and for that purpose they must
be taught to feel and to think. We cannot begin teaching reading
and writing until the child has acquired some general knowledge
and speaking knowledge of language. The study and teaching of
language were analyzed by Pestalozzi into three divisions: the
study of sounds and words, grammar and sentence structure, and
the study of speech. It is the mother's duty, prior to the child's
entering school, to encourage him to speak and to experiment
with sound, and she should also have taught him the names of all
the common objects around him. Grammatical rules should be
taught at the end of the study of language, not at the beginning.

Language was reduced by Pestalozzi to words or names, and
these to sounds. Formal exercises were constructed for each
stage, beginning with syllables. Pestalozzi's method was to take
from the dictionary the names of certain common things and also
words that described striking qualities possessed by those things,
nouns and adjectives, as a basis for a lesson—e.g., the evening is
peaceful, cheerful, cool, rainy. Pestalozzi required his pupils to
memorize the names of the most important objects in nature, history, and geography and then to form sentences in various ways
incorporating the words. For such exercises in language, Pestalozzi used both objects and pictures.

Pestalozzi experimented in the application of his principles to
the teaching of Latin and other foreign languages. Guimps records that "he considered the best means of teaching a foreign
language to be that which nature employs in teaching a child to
speak its mother-tongue, *viz.*, constant practice in the spoken
language. It was thus that, with the addition of a little grammar,
the Germans learned French, and the French learned German,
most successfully, at Yverdon."[31] In his *Swan Song*, Pestalozzi asserts that "a child soon learns to speak a foreign language even
from an illiterate person, who merely talks to him without any

attempt at instruction; but he does not do this with a skillful teacher who adopts the mechanical grammatical method."[32]

VII *History*

It was Pestalozzi's conviction that history did not belong in the lower elementary curriculum, and that it was unwise to attempt to teach historical incidents and their causes and effects to young children. His firm stand on the matter was based on the argument that children lack knowledge of the world around them and therefore cannot judge peoples and nations in another age and another place. Further, Pestalozzi objected to history on the ground that it exposes innocent children to learning about the wickedness and evils of the world before they are able to understand their significance. Because of such prejudices and lack of interest, history was a largely neglected field in the Pestalozzian institutes, restricted to lists of major persons and accounts of events that might be useful at later stages

VIII *Physical Education and Manual Training*

The development of the body had great importance in the total system of education designed by Pestalozzi. For maximum development of his powers, equal attention must be paid to a child's mental, moral, and physical capacities. Of these three fundamental aspects of education, physical education was most neglected in Pestalozzi's time. The schools for the poor regarded physical training as a frivolous waste of time, and any indulgence in physical exercises and sporting activities as irresponsible.

Pestalozzi's treatise *Concerning Physical Education* stresses the need for physical education as a part of a child's total development. Beginning in the home, the mother teaches the child to stand, to walk, and to go through other simple physical exercises. The father later extends the training by making the child jump over blocks, climb trees, slide on the ice, throw projectiles, and swing whips. Too frequently, however, these excellent first steps were not continued in the schools, where, according to Pestalozzi, the children "are barely allowed to twitch. That which is being done for their minds is given such unnatural importance that if a child so much as moves its hands and feet it forces the poor schoolmaster off the rails."[33]

Ideally, in Pestalozzi's view, the school should try to widen the range of a child's muscular activity, meanwhile maintaining the natural harmony between the mental, spiritual, and physical. A wide range of gymnastic exercises and games of increasing difficulty should build up the child's muscles, to make them flexible, strong, and agile. Apart from these attributes, it was held that physical education develops the moral qualities of perseverance and courage. "Gymnastics, well conducted," wrote Pestalozzi, "essentially contribute to render children not only cheerful and healthy, which, for moral education, are two all-important points, but also to promote among them a certain spirit of union, and a brotherly feeling, which is most gratifying to the observer." He added that regular gymnastic exercises develop "habits of industry, openness and frankness of character, personal courage, and manly conduct in suffering pain."[34]

The physical training and work at Yverdon was described by Guimps:

When the weather was favorable, some hours in the afternoon were given every week to military exercises. . . . Gymnastics, prisoner's-base and other games went on regularly. There was skating as well in the winter; and in summer, bathing in the lake and mountain excursions. The first day of spring was celebrated every year by a walk on the neighboring heights. . . . The pupils formed a little regiment of their own. . . . They soon learned to go through the most complicated maneuvers with wonderful precision.[35]

A high educational value was placed on manual training by Pestalozzi. The school at Bonnal, described in *Leonard and Gertrude*, is an industrial school. In his *Christopher and Elizabeth* (1782), Pestalozzi writes: "If I had time and patience and could be a village schoolmaster, I would take spinning-wheels and weaving stools into my school, and the children should learn to speak, to read, and to reckon, whilst their hands were busily employed. . . . Every day the schoolmaster realized more fully how work cultivates the intelligence, gives force to the feelings of the heart, and keeps alive the sense of duty."[36] These convictions were unchanged by the passage of time, for some years later Pestalozzi added: "I now regard it as a clear and incontrovertible principle, that man is much more truly educated through that which he does than through that which he learns."[37]

In his advocacy of manual training and vocational education, Pestalozzi differentiated between poor children and children of the well-to-do. Realistically he recognized that the children of poor parents would be required to help support the family. The skills which they should develop in school therefore ought to fit the family's social and economic station. But general education must not be neglected. Vocational education as seen by Pestalozzi was simply one phase of the education of the whole man. Writing of the agricultural and industrial program at Neuhof, he stated: "But, however much I felt that my institution required this, I was no less convinced that every vocational training which did not provide the individual with a commensurate cultivation of the head and the heart would not only be inadequate but would be unworthy and would degrade him to the status of one slavishly trained merely for making a living.[38]

Vocational education under the Pestalozzian plan was divided into three major work areas: agriculture, handicrafts, and industry. During this period, agriculture was an essential part of the Swiss economy. Handicraft production was widespread, though beginning to give way to the factory system and mass production. Going against the tide, Pestalozzi believed that domestic training and handicraft production should be preserved, contending that "home happiness, home industry, and home manners" could counteract the detrimental aspects of the factory system.

Manual work was done intermittently by the pupils at Yverdon, though it never became a part of the regular program. Of the various occupations pursued, gardening proved the most successful. Guimps notes, "Sometimes the pupils had a little patch of their own to cultivate; sometimes they were told off in twos and threes to work for a few hours, under the direction of the gardener. They did fairly well at bookbinding and cardboard work; they also made solids for the study of geometry."[39]

IX *Conclusion*

In a highly perceptive comment, Hermann Krüsi observed that "in applying his principles of education to specific branches, Pestalozzi often wandered from the true path; but running through all are philosophic ideas worthy of the great fame of their author."[40] A serious weakness in Pestalozzi's method was the neglect of history and literature. He did little or nothing for humanistic studies. History is mentioned by him only occasionally in discussing education, and literature is scarcely mentioned at all. The reason for the neglect was doubtless the long-range influence of Rousseau, dating from his youth, and the revolt led by Rousseau against the "bookishness" of the Renaissance. Biographies and stirring tales which could have enriched instruction and provided concrete illustrations were simply omitted in the Pestalozzi method.

CHAPTER 6

Culmination

THE last twenty years of Pestalozzi's active career as an educator and schoolmaster, 1805 to 1825, were spent at Yverdon. Here he reached the summit of his fame and ultimately experienced his most severe disappointments. Pestalozzi's ideas were beginning to triumph throughout Europe, to his tremendous gratification, but at home he continued to be plagued by failures as an administrator, a too-confiding nature, and an absolute lack of any sense of the practical.

The castle at Yverdon was built on a Roman site, and had formerly been a stronghold of the Dukes of Savoy. It had come under the control of the municipal government, which repaired the structure and turned it over for Pestalozzi's use for life, rent free. The space was ample, with large halls for classrooms and assemblies, dormitories, and wide passages. The furnishings were simple but adequate. For playgrounds, there were a large courtyard, broad avenues, and a nearby meadow. A half-mile away was Lake Neuchâtel.

The work of the institute at Yverdon was a continuation and culmination of the plans first developed at Stans and Burgdorf. It immediately became a center for educational experimentation to such an extent it would be fair to state that practically every concept or method found in modern elementary education had at least rudimentary beginnings in the Yverdon setting. The keynote in teaching all subjects was observation connected with language. The children were taught to observe correctly, to recognize the relations of things, and accordingly to have no difficulty in expressing clearly what they thoroughly understood.

Initially there were seventy pupils enrolled at Yverdon. By 1809 that figure had more than doubled. Eventually the number of residents reached 250—pupils, teachers, servants, and

Pestalozzi's family. It was a truly cosmopolitan group: Swiss, Germans, French, Italians, Spaniards, Russians, and Americans. In addition, there were day pupils from Yverdon, boarders of branch institutes opened in the town, and later pupils from a newly founded girls' school. The age span represented among the children was from about six to twelve. A majority of the boys came from middle-class homes, but a number of non-fee-paying poor children were admitted. Regardless of social background, all children were regarded and treated as equals. Emphasis was placed on providing a natural environment, with fresh-air exercise, nourishing food, and physical care. As specified, the program's objectives were "order and regularity, exertion without overstraining, alternation between lessons and games and between one subject of learning and another."[1] It was a regimen designed to ensure the children's health and happiness.

A teacher at the girls' school, Eduard Biber, gives the following eyewitness account of the general spirit prevailing in the Yverdon institute during its best period:

The pupils and teachers were united by that unaffected love which Pestalozzi, who, in years, was a man verging to the grave, but in heart and mind a genuine child, seemed to breathe out continually and impart to all who came within his influence. The children forgot that they had another home, and the teachers that there was any other world than the Institution. Not a man claimed a privilege for himself, not one wished to he considered above the others. Teachers and pupils were entirely united. They not only slept in the same rooms, and shared the labors and enjoyments of the day, but they were on a footing of perfect equality. The same man who read a lecture on History one hour, would, perhaps, during the next, sit on the same form with the pupils for a lesson in Arithmetic or Geometry, and without compromising his dignity, would even request their assistance and receive their hints.[2]

Another associate, Hermann Krüsi, noted that Pestalozzi had great influence over his teachers. Twice weekly he met with them in the evenings to discuss their work. At those meetings, each individual was asked to give an account of his lesson plans and of the character and behavior of the children placed under his special care. According to Krüsi, "These consultations tended to produce unity of feeling, thought, and action among the teachers," helping to correct mistakes and giving all an opportunity to profit from successful methods developed by individuals.[3] Too, the characters and habits of the pupils became known to everyone.

Physical education in the institute received full attention. The pupils were required to rise early, their food was wholesome, nutritious, and abundant, and gymnastic exercises were practiced systematically throughout the year. Favorite amusements in summer were bathing in the neighboring lake and walks in the hills. The location, amid some of the most beautiful scenery in Europe, was also stimulating to students and teachers. The castle commanded an extensive view of Lake Neuchâtel; to the west the Jura mountains formed an unbroken chain, and to the south lay a wide, rich valley.

Pestalozzi was overjoyed at the international recognition being accorded his school and set himself a superhuman work schedule in a desire to meet all expectations. He rose at two o'clock in the morning to engage in writing. The same zeal was expected of his colleagues, who did their share of the housework, chopped wood, lit the fires, and copied manuscripts, when they were not occupied in teaching. An assistant, Johannes Ramsauer, related that "there were years when not one of us would have been found in bed after three o'clock in the morning, and we worked summer and winter from three to six o'clock."[4]

The routine established for the children was almost equally Spartan. They rose at half-past five and began their first lesson at six. Morning prayer followed at seven and afterwards the children washed in the courtyard, did their toilets, and ate a breakfast consisting of soup. Lessons resumed at eight o'clock. During a recess at ten, fruit and bread were provided by the housekeeper. At midday, an hour's recreation was allowed for bathing or a game of prisoner's base. Dinner at one o'clock consisted of soup, meat, and vegetables. Lessons began again at one-thirty and continued until half-past four. Then came the afternoon meal either of cheese and fruit or bread and butter, followed by a period of recreation until six o'clock, when the last hour of classes was scheduled. Supper was set for eight o'clock, after which there was a period of evening prayer. The children were in bed by nine o'clock. A total of ten lessons daily was prescribed, though with occasional breaks, such as long walks on Wednesday and Sunday afternoons and afternoon sessions of military drills. On Sunday mornings the children attended church in the town.

Vulliemin, the historian, a pupil under Pestalozzi at Yverdon, recollected: "The castle was built in the shape of a huge square, and its great rooms and courts were admirably adapted for the games as well as the studies of a large school. Within its walls were assembled from a hundred and fifty to two hundred children of all nations, who divided their time between lessons and happy play. It often happened that a game of prisoner's base, begun in the castle court, would be finished on the grass near the lake. In winter we used to make a mighty snow-fortress, which was attacked and defended with equal heroism."[5]

A short time after the opening of the Yverdon institute, Pestalozzi prepared and published a *Report to Parents and to the Public*, dealing with the work and condition of the school. The document is valuable in revealing the ideals Pestalozzi and his staff were following and in presenting an authoritative account of the actual organization of the institute. The report corrects the impression that the school was only for young boys between eight and ten and that it was meant only for children of the higher classes. Facts on the curriculum were stated: German and French were taught and boys who wished could learn Latin and Greek. Other subjects offered were geography, natural history (experimental and descriptive), history, literature, arithmetic, geometry, surveying, drawing, writing, and singing. Further, the report considers at length the moral and physical well-being of the boys and the special care taken to adapt instruction to the individual nature of the pupils.

Pestalozzi's time was fully occupied in the superintendence of the complex Yverdon institute, attending to its financial management, carrying on an extensive correspondence, and engaging in literary activities. As in previous enterprises with which he had been associated, he showed little taste or aptitude for administrative or financial affairs. At least one-third of the pupils enrolled at Yverdon paid little or none of their board and tuition. No pupil was rejected on account of his poverty, however, and everyone who manifested a desire to learn and to improve was admitted. As Krüsi commented, "Although urged to caution by the sad experiences of his early life, Pestalozzi ever forgot his worldly interests when the welfare of humanity appealed to his susceptible heart."[6]

Because of their sketchy education and experience, in most instances, the young teachers were incapable of applying Pestalozzian principles in uniform ways or with true understanding. Writing in later years, Vulliemin concluded, "What was so emphatically called Pestolozzi's *method* was an enigma to us [the students]. So it was to our teachers. Like the disciples of Socrates, every one of them interpreted the master's doctrines in his own fashion; but we were far from the times when these divergencies created discord, when our chief masters, after having each one of them laid claim to be the only one who really understood Pestalozzi, ended by declaring that Pestalozzi did not really understand himself."[7]

Another serious practical difficulty was that two different languages, German and French, had to be spoken. In 1809, about 60 percent of the pupils were Swiss and the remainder were Germans, French, Russians, Italians, Spaniards, Americans, and English. Nine of the fifteen teachers were Swiss. Of thirty-two persons studying Pestalozzi's method, only seven were Swiss. Karl von Raumer noted that "with such a medley of children, the institution was devoid of a predominant mother-tongue, and assumed the mongrel character of a border-province. Pestalozzi read the prayers every morning and evening, first in German, then in French! I found French children who did not understand the most common German word."[8]

A further obstacle to thorough and successful instruction was the interruptions and distractions of many visitors. A critical comment on that matter came from Johannes Ramsauer, a teaching assistant: "It was nothing unusual in summer for strangers to come to the castle four or five times in the same day, and for us to have to interrupt the instruction to expound the method to them."[9] Pupils were sometimes taken to the hotel at which an important personage was staying, so that a demonstration might be given to him.

During the years in which the Yverdon institute operated, it attracted numerous teaching assistants, some of whom were subsequently to make a deep imprint on European education. Ultimately, the success or failure of the school hinged upon the caliber and personality of these individuals. Pestalozzi's failure to

maintain harmony among certain strong-minded masters resulted
in the end in the collapse of the institute.

Outstanding among Pestalozzi's associates at Yverdon were two
men: Johannes Niederer and Joseph Schmid. Niederer had been
born in a poor home in Appenzell. While still in his twenties, he
joined Pestalozzi at Burgdorf and followed him to Yverdon. Silber
describes Niederer as "a young man with bright blue eyes, red
hair, and a high, stubborn brow, . . . very intelligent, ambitious,
and headstrong, and well trained in philosophy and divinity."[10]
He gave up a pastorate to serve as Protestant minister and
teacher of Scripture in the Burgdorf institute. Immediately, Niederer became one of the chief masters at Yverdon, and by his
lively mind, lucidity in expressing ideas in speaking and writing,
and university education exerted great influence on Pestalozzi
himself. Niederer had charge of religious instruction in the upper
classes and also gave lectures on the method and assisted Pestalozzi by editing his literary work. With his philosophical background, Niederer became spokesman for Pestalozzi, expounding
his ideas and defending him from adverse criticism. In time,
however, their theories tended to diverge, and, as Pestalozzi remarked, Niederer "created his own system on the idea of
elementary education."[11] So dominant did Niederer become at
Yverdon that Pestalozzi ironically suggested on one occasion, "I
no longer understand myself; if you want to know what I think
and what I wish, go and ask Niederer."[12] At Yverdon, Niederer
revised everything that Pestalozzi wrote for publication and corrected the chief defects, but at the same time destroyed to some
extent the originality of matter and form.

Joseph Schmid, another strong personality, was determined to
counteract Niederer's dominant status. Schmid was a shepherd
boy from the Tyrol who came to Pestalozzi at Burgdorf completely lacking in formal education. Upon completion of his work
as a student at Burgdorf, Pestalozzi had persuaded him to remain
as a teacher. Because of their close association as student and
teacher, Schmid had a special place in Pestalozzi's heart. The
former was a hard, practical man, whose administrative abilities
were valuable in the operation of the institute. As a teacher he
showed a remarkable talent for mathematics, which he taught
with skill and success. His textbook, *Elementary Lessons in
Number and Form*, was one of the most important books to come

out of the Yverdon experiment. In personality, however, Schmid appeared to leave much to be desired. A harsh verdict on Schmid was expressed by Roger de Guimps, a contemporary: "With a glance like an eagle and a will of iron, he was crafty, domineering, and utterly devoid of sensibility. He gradually obtained complete ascendancy over Pestalozzi's mind, and was finally the cause of the departure of the other masters, and the ruin of the institute."[13]

Pestalozzi's obvious admiration for, confidence in, and favoritism toward Schmid were highly displeasing to Niederer, who was persuaded with difficulty by Pestalozzi to remain when, in 1816, Krüsi and fifteen other masters resigned in protest against Schmid's authoritarian regime. Schmid had resigned in 1810, but had been brought back from Austria, where he had gone to head a school, because of the need for his administrative and organizing skills at Yverdon.

In 1809, Pestalozzi requested an official inspection of the institute in the hope that his method would be recommended for adoption as the basis for a national system of education. In part, too, Pestalozzi felt that an impartial inquiry into the conduct and efficiency of the school was demanded because of the numerous attacks being made on it in the Swiss newspapers and by other hostile elements. Apparently on Niederer's advice, therefore, but contrary to Schmid's strongly expressed doubts, Pestalozzi addressed himself to the Helvetian government to ask "that it would deign to give a public mark of attention either to the institute at Yverdon, or to the method of elementary education there in use, which having obtained the suffrages of several states and of a great number of learned and highly respected men, now attracts the attention of all Europe."[14]

Pestalozzi's petition was approved and a commission of three members was appointed to make the inspection: Mérian, a member of the executive council of the canton of Basle; Trechsel, professor of mathematics at Bern; and Father Gregoire Girard, director of the schools at Fribourg. The commission paid a five-day visit to the institute in November, 1809, during which it refused to take into account the aims and principles of the work but confined itself entirely to a consideration of the results achieved. Father Girard was assigned the task of preparing a report. When that document finally appeared in print the following year it did

full justice to the nobility of Pestalozzi's character and purpose
and found much worthy of praise in the teaching of individual
staff members. On the whole, however, the tone of the
commission's report was critical, and the conclusion was reached
that what was good in the institute's work was not new and what
was new had serious defects. The principles on which education
at Yverdon were based, "the invariable maxims of goodness and
beneficence," had not been invented by Pestalozzi nor been
claimed by him to be original. In the application of the method to
various branches of instruction, Father Girard found nothing particularly novel, except in the teaching of drawing and singing.
The good results achieved in the teaching of mathematics were
acknowledged. Also, the charge of irreligion against the institute
was refuted. To the question of whether the method should be
introduced in schools throughout the country, the answer was in
the negative. Despite the successes of Pestalozzianism, the
commission's judgment was that it should not be set up as an example for all of Switzerland to admire and emulate. The effect of
the report was that, though the national assembly expressed by
resolution the thanks of the nation to Pestalozzi, all hope of Yverdon becoming a state institution for the training of teachers was
destroyed.

The commission's findings caused great distress among the
Yverdon staff. Pestalozzi felt strongly that the five-day visit had
been too brief to give an accurate impression and that justice had
not been done to his institute. A long-drawn-out literary feud followed, as friends and foes of the school resorted to the newspapers, pamphlets, and books to present their sides of the controversy. The government report had provided Pestalozzi's
enemies with ammunition for open attacks. A vitriolic assault, for
example, was made by a Bernese professor of constitutional law,
K. L. von Haller, who accused Pestalozzi of being a revolutionary
and an anarchist. Niederer was the principal spokesman for the
defense. A printing press was set up in the castle for the production and distribution of polemic publications; the end result of the
press operation was serious financial difficulties for the institute.
As Holman points out, "The greatest possible mischief had been
done to the fair fame of the institution, and public opinion and
confidence had received a severe shock, in consequence of the
newspaper and controversial writings connected with these
quarrels."[15]

Since 1810 the financial problems of the institute had been in-creasing. This was the principal reason for recalling the business-like Schmid from Austria in 1815 to use his practical ability to bring order to a situation quite out of control. Schmid insisted, however, upon being more than a business manager, and at once attempted to assume control over every aspect of the life at Yver-don. Strict discipline replaced the freedom formerly enjoyed by the staff. In Krüsi's words, "the lower civil servants had, as un-questioning agents, to carry out the orders of higher officials."[16] Schmid paid off the institute's debts, dismissed some staff mem-bers, reduced the salaries of the others, and increased their teaching hours. After the death in 1815 of Frau Pestalozzi, who had had a calming influence on the school's warring elements, matters rapidly deteriorated.

As early as 1806, the Yverdon school had branched out with a separate institute for girls. With his strong convictions concerning the importance of preschool education of young children and the vital role of the mother, Pestalozzi had always possessed a keen desire to provide present and future mothers with proper training to meet their educational duties. In his original establishments at Stans and Neuhof, designed mainly for poor children, boys and girls had been educated together, family style. At Yverdon, where the pupils were predominantly middle-class, admission was restricted to boys. As the demand grew for educational facilities for middle-class girls, a separate house was opened in Yverdon, with Krüsi as director, his sister Elisabeth as teacher, and Pestalozzi's daughter-in-law as housekeeper. The curriculum was similar to that for the boys' school, except that woodwork was re-placed by feminine types of handwork. Later, a well-trained headmistress, Rosette Kasthofer, developed the establishment into a flourishing institute for the higher education of girls, and in 1813 it became independent.

Pestalozzi's optimistic, ever-hopeful nature was seldom daunted, even in the midst of adversity and discord. In 1818, he fulfilled a long-time ambition by establishing a poor school at Clindy, a hamlet near Yverdon. At the beginning, there were twelve pupils, all neglected children. The plan of organization was the same as for the original poor-school at Neuhof. According to Pestalozzi, the children "were to be brought up as poor boys and receive that kind of instruction which is suitable for the poor, including, amongst other things, chopping wood and carting manure."[17] Here at the age of seventy-two, Pestalozzi repeated his greatest personal success. The school's reputation spread and soon there were thirty pupils. But gradually, with what Pestalozzi described as his "unrivaled incapacity to govern," he allowed the curriculum to be brought into line with that of the institute, other teachers began to take part in the work, paying pupils were admitted, the school's character changed, and eventually it was transferred to the Yverdon institute. On March 17, 1824, a statement from Pestalozzi read, "I announced my total inability further to fulfil the expectations and hopes which I had excited, by my projected poor school, in the hearts of so many philanthropists and friends of education."[18]

A year later came the end. Broken by internal dissention and crushed by debt, the Yverdon institute had to be closed. The final blow was struck by the dismissal of Schmid, obtained by his enemies from the Council of State, in the form of a decree of expulsion from Switzerland, dated October 6, 1824, exiling him to his native Austria. Pestalozzi returned to Neuhof, to the farm he still owned, where exactly half a century before his first poor-school had been started. For the last two years of his life he wrote extensively, including the *Swan Song*, in which he presents a final statement of his views on education, and *My Fortunes as Superintendent of My Educational Establishments at Burgdorf and Yverdon*, in which he reviews the events that occurred in those institutions. For the Helvetian Society, of which Pestalozzi had been elected president, he wrote an address *On Fatherland and Education*, and in the same year, 1826, he presented a paper to the Society for the Promotion of Education, entitled *Attempt at a Sketch on the Essence of the Idea of Elementary Education*, dealing with the simplest methods of educating children from infancy to the sixth year. In addition to these activities, he was writing the fifth volume of *Leonard and Gertrude*, a new *Manual for Mothers*, and a book of elementary exercises designed to teach children Latin in the same way that they learn their mother tongue.

In the midst of his literary activities, Pestalozzi was working vigorously on his ever-cherished plan of a revived poor school at Neuhof, and he regularly taught in the village school at Birr.

The publication of *My Fortunes* aroused some of the old controversies. Pestalozzi's defense of Schmid therein antagonized

Niederer, who had left the institute in 1817, and there were fresh press attacks on Pestalozzi, who was attempting to write replies to the criticisms when he became violently ill and died on February 17, 1827.

Twenty years after Pestalozzi's death, a bust of him was placed in a niche in the church wall above his grave, with the following epitaph:

Here rests Heinrich Pestalozzi, born at Zurich on the 12th of January, 1746, died at Brugg on the 17th of February, 1827. Saviour of the poor at Neuhof, preacher to the people in *Leonard and Gertrude*, father of the orphans at Stans, founder of the new elementary school in Burgdorf and Münchenbuchsee, educator of humanity at Yverdon. Man, Christian, citizen. Everything for others, nothing for himself! Blessings on his name! TO OUR FATHER PESTALOZZI, Grateful Aargau.

The decline and fall of the Yverdon institute can be attributed to various factors. Most important, probably, was Pestalozzi's inability to maintain harmony among his associates. Hardly less significant was the old bugbear that seemed to dog all Pestalozzian enterprises, financial insecurity. On the other hand, in perspective, the Burgdorf and Yverdon institutes may be accounted successful because they were free of rigid organization and strict discipline, a feature that attracted assistants and students to Pestalozzi. His own attitude is well expressed in this statement: "My opinion is that such a society can only succeed if each member of it is free to go astray and to make mistakes, and is able rather through quiet experience than correction to realize himself and to make as much progress as his own character allows of."[19]

A recent biographer, Michael Heafford, concludes that "if Pestalozzi could have known that the principles of education which he had expounded would be universally acknowledged, he would gladly have accepted all the failures and misfortunes of the final years of his life. His own assessment of his life would rest, as ours must too, on whether these principles are as universal and as valid as he himself believed."[20]

CHAPTER 7

Methods Of Elementary Education

T HROUGHOUT Pestalozzian literature there are frequent references to Pestalozzi's "method," as though it were a fully defined and developed set of principles, capable of universal application. In fact, the methods are highly amorphous, varying in time and place.

Eduard Biber, an early associate, points out that "At the opening of his school at Stans Pestalozzi had no plan of lessons, no method, no school book, except one, and even this he scarcely used at all. Nor did he attempt to form a plan, to sketch out a method, or to compose a book. The only object of his attention was to find out at each moment what instruction his children stood particularly in need of, and what was the best manner of connecting it with the knowledge they already possessed, or deducing it from the observations which they had an opportunity of making within the sphere of their daily life."[1] The proceedings were entirely unsystematic, according to Biber, but though lacking in method, "the children felt attracted, interested, stimulated." Even at this early stage, however, when the Stans experiment ended after twelve months, Pestalozzi's mind was filled with numerous ideas concerning ways and means for continuing his educational activities.

A later commentator, the French educator Gabriel Compayré, adds further clarification:

The teaching of Pestalozzi was in reality a long groping in unexplored ways—a ceaseless searching after the best methods. Following his pedagogic instinct, his loving desire to please and develop the child's mind, and availing himself of the immediate practical skill of such assistants as were at his command (most of them young, and pupil-teachers who hac come to study his system), he never worked out his own theories to complete satisfaction or clearly formulated them in manuals for the guidance of others.[2]

Nevertheless, a thread of consistency runs through Pestalozzi's voluminous writings on education. To some extent the principles in which he believed were a continuation of Rousseau's naturalism. But unlike Rousseau, Pestalozzi did not attempt to glorify the state of nature as a utopia. On the contrary, he recognized that nature in the raw is often brutish, and that primitive man was as fierce and cruel as any jungle beast. Thus, Pestalozzi rejected Rousseau's vague romantic dreams of the happy savage living in a sylvan paradise. The second stage of man, Pestalozzi held, is that of society, which becomes an absolute necessity because man's animal instincts and drives have to be tamed and controlled. There follow the origin and enforcement of laws and the creation of religion, the setting up of certain taboos and restrictions and the seeking to define right and wrong. These efforts are often defective, however, for society may enforce the wrong kind of laws and protect the guilty to the disadvantage of the innocent.

According to Pestalozzi's philosophy, mankind has three forces at work, all simultaneously and each to be found in every individual: primitive impulses, social instincts, and ethical yearnings. The primary device for overcoming animal impulses and achieving an ethical, moral society is education, but education directed toward inward development rather than artificial training.

In one important respect, Pestalozzi accepted Rousseau's naturalistic teachings. His first writing, *The Evening Hours of a Hermit*, held that "all the beneficent powers of man are due to neither art nor chance, but to nature," and that education should follow "the course laid down by nature."[3] In this and other works, Pestalozzi draws an analogy between a child's development and that of the natural growth of a plant or animal, as for example in the following statement:

Sound education stands before me symbolized by a tree planted near fertilizing waters. A little seed, which contains the design of the tree, its form and proportions, is placed in the soil. See how it germinates and expands into trunk, branches, leaves, flowers, and fruit. The whole tree is an uninterrupted chain of organic parts, the plan of which existed in its seed and root. Man is similar to the tree. In the new-born child are hidden those faculties which are to unfold during life. The individual and separate organs of his being form themselves gradually into unison, and build up humanity in the image of God.[4]

In line with this concept of the laws of nature, education was defined by Pestalozzi as "the natural, progressive, and harmonious development of all the powers and capacities of the human being." Further, "the knowledge to which the child is to be led by instruction must, therefore, be subjected to a certain order of succession, the beginning of which must be adapted to the first unfolding of his powers, and the progress kept exactly parallel to that of his development."[5]

Pestalozzi's criticisms of the prevailing educational methods of his time were especially directed toward the fact that they were out of harmony with nature. The traditional practices, he maintained, gave the pupil a mere ability to read words, a memory knowledge of mathematics, and a superficial, largely useless, culture through the classics. "Our unpsychological schools," Pestalozzi asserted, "are essentially only artificial stifling machines for destroying all the results of the power and experience that nature herself brings to life."[6]

Pestalozzi modified and extended Rousseau's educational doctrine by urging the education of all children, regardless of their circumstances and abilities. Rousseau was concerned in *Emile* solely with the education of young aristocrats. It was Pestalozzi's contention that poverty could be relieved and society reformed only by the mental and moral development of all persons. Accordingly, he was a steadfast advocate of universal education.

I *Significance of the Home in the Educational Process*

Pestalozzi was convinced that a child's education began from the moment of his birth. From the beginning, every day in a child's life and every source of influence plays a part in forming his character and personality. It could be regarded as a truism, therefore, that the first years of a child's existence spent in the home environment are an essential element of his education—in some respects more basic than the later school years, for it is in the home that the foundation is laid upon which education in the school must be built. The mother's voice is the first to reach the child in his cradle. She speaks to him as she nurses, feeds, and dresses him. The constant association in an atmosphere of love creates a lasting impression on the child. Home is the only place where a child can live a complete life, a microcosm of the larger social world outside. As Pestalozzi states, "It is only in the holiness of home that the equal development of all the human faculties can be directed, managed, and assured; and it is from this point that educational efforts must be conducted, if education, as a national affair, is to have real reference to the wants of the people, and is to cause, by its influence, the coinciding of external human knowledge, power, and motives with the internal, everlasting, divine essence of our nature."[7]

Pestalozzian reform, therefore, is solidly grounded in the principle of the education of the child in the home, for the home, through the home, and by the home. The child's primary education is for the purpose of making him a dutiful and efficient member of the family; otherwise, he will not become a dutiful and efficient member of society.

Constantly stressed by Pestalozzi is the power of love in education. For the child, the love relationship with his mother provides a climate of emotional security. If a child is given love and care by his mother, he will develop into a person capable of giving and receiving love. As the reverse of the coin, if love is absent from the family circle, the frustrated, unloved child will grow into a selfish, emotionally disturbed adult.

The home as seen by Pestalozzi served a double function. In the first place, it protected the child from the outside world, providing security and sheltering him from detrimental influences, and, second, it furnished a background for his moral, intellectual, and physical development.

As noted earlier, Pestalozzi himself was brought up entirely in the care and under the influence of women. His mother, a shy, retiring woman, left a widow in straitened circumstances at an early age, could not have managed her children without the help of their devoted servant, Barbara. Pestalozzi expressed in moving terms what "Babeli" meant to him. Because of her faithfulness, the child grew and developed under the loving care of a devoted woman. The fact that this woman was only a simple servant impressed Pestalozzi, and he attributed his love and devotion to people and his belief in their innate goodness and abilities to this early experience. The experience was repeated later in the person of Lisabeth, another loyal servant, who came to offer her services to the Pestalozzi family after the disastrous failure at Neuhof. Without wages or rewards, Lisabeth brought order and cleanliness to the estate, cared for the family members, and soon became their irreplaceable and untiring friend and helper. Even in literary matters, Pestalozzi valued her advice, for, he wrote, "she was a very clever woman although uneducated."[8]

Leonard and Gertrude incorporates most of Pestalozzi's later ideas on education, social reform, economics, and politics. The character of Gertrude in the novel personifies his theory that the family is the center of society, education starts in the home, and the mother is the child's first teacher. Institutions, which are merely inadequate substitutes, should be modeled after home life, following the road the mother takes by instinct. Pestalozzi's idea of elementary education started from the view that mankind's salvation must depend upon the regeneration of the home and the perfection of home education. This was the running theme in his two most famous works, *Leonard and Gertrude* and *How Gertrude Teaches Her Children*. The latter was intended as a guide to mothers for instructing their children at home.

As elementary education continues under the schoolmaster, there should be no deviation from the principles of sound home methods, Pestalozzi insisted, as his description of the Burgdorf institute brings out:

Our house had, in order to attain its aims, to become a place of fatherly education, rather than one of public instruction. Cheerfulness, child-like devotion, open trust, refuge in the arms of the teacher as in the mother's arms, and the training of all forms of obedience, of perseverance, and of self-control to be achieved in their cheerfulness and through their devotion: on these we wished to lay the foundation of our house—in contrast to the opinion of the world which at present judges every educational institution primarily on the results of its instructional methods.[9]

In his *Swan Song*, Pestalozzi traces how the seeds of love, confidence, gratitude, brotherly feeling, patience, obedience, and sense of duty develop in the child's mind and heart through the tender care of his mother and by family intercourse.

II Anschauung

In the course of his efforts to develop a natural system of education, Pestalozzi adopted as a central principle the German word

Anschauung, translated variously as observation, intuition, contemplation, sense experience, perception, and sense impression. As used by Pestalozzi, the term may be defined as a face-to-face experience of the realities of the universe—minerals, plants, animals, mental or moral phenomena, historical persons or events, etc. It was Pestalozzi's belief that *Anschauung* is the foundation of all knowledge. The doctrine may be summed up in two phrases: "Things before words" and "Concrete before abstract." In his own estimation, *Anschauung* was Pestalozzi's most important contribution to educational theory, and practical applications of the concept were made in virtually all branches of instruction: arithmetic, drawing, geography, physical sciences, nature study, reading, and even the teaching of morals and religion. The principle was that actual sensory experience, carefully organized and systematically worked out, is the only sound basis of instruction.

Anschauung as conceived by Pestalozzi involved a radical change from traditional methods of teaching. Previously, from the very outset of a child's studies, he had been presented with abstract and general ideas, for which he had no basis of personal experience. He may have been told of rivers and oceans, without ever having seen either; of mountains and river basins, without having climbed even a hill. He was taught the words "duty" and "virtue" before becoming aware of the meaning of moral sentiments. It was such superficial instruction, typical of the old "monastic" schools, that Pestalozzi wished to sweep away. And that is why he discarded books and rejected didactic lessons. Instead, his aim was to place the child in the presence of objects. "The child of my method feels his power only in surroundings that are real to him," Pestalozzi asserted. "He is not puffed out with empty learned words which have no background in his experience."[10]

The essential laws of instruction depend, according to Pestalozzi's theory, upon observing three things: (1) to teach the child to look upon everything that is brought before him as a unit, e.g., how many and what kinds of objects are in front of him; (2) to teach the child to recognize the appearance, form, or outline of these objects; and (3) as soon as possible to make the child acquainted with all the words and names descriptive of objects known to him.

"The man who in his youth has not caught butterflies, nor

wandered over hill and dale hunting for plants, etc., in spite of
all desk work, will not get far in his subject," declared Pestalozzi.
"He will always be exposed to blunders which otherwise he
would never have made."[11] Definitions not founded on sense impression, he added, produce a funguslike wisdom, which dies
rapidly in the sunlight.

The importance the great Swiss educator attached to object
lessons—e.g., geometrical models, field trips, rock collections, or
a hot stove—derives from the Pestalozzian concept of how a child
perceives and learns. By way of the pedagogical method Pestalozzi called *Anschauung,* one could develop a child's or even an
infant's powers of perception and intuition, and thus pave the
way to further learning and instruction. Any mother could be
shown, Pestalozzi believed, how best to train her infant's powers
of observation, touch, taste, sight, and smell. The identical principle could be applied throughout the child's school years, with
apparently amazing results. A child who has been reared and
trained in this fashion will be ready in the future for the scientific
pursuit of any branch of knowledge.

Despite his trust in nature and natural development, Pestalozzi
never held that learning should not be carefully guided. In his
Letters to Gessner, he reiterates over and over that the child
must be led "from confused intuition to clear perception," to be
raised "from vague intuition to precise idea." In short, nature's
education is incomplete and insufficient and must be com-
plemented and rounded out by methodically arranged exercises.
Pestalozzi's method called for the various elements which compose elementary education to be offered to the child "in continuous, unbroken succession." There is no disposition to hurry the
child; on the contrary, he is held back deliberately on each exercise until he has achieved thorough mastery of it. Only then is he
permitted to take a step forward, i.e., after the preceding knowledge is completely acquired. Pestalozzi claimed to follow nature's
order in grading the exercises developed to support his method.
The essential principle was to proceed from the near to the
remote—building first upon the child's observation of things
touched and seen around him, in his immediate neighborhood,
and going from there "in ever widening circles" to more distant
objects.

In a brief recapitulation of his pedagogic theories, Pestalozzi wrote: "For each branch of knowledge there should be series of exercises having their starting-point within reach of all (intuition), and with a regular sequence (gradation), which would keep the child's faculties constantly at work, without exhausting or even tiring them, and would contribute to continuous, easy, and attractive progress."[12] The faculties are developed and strengthened by exercise, from which the conclusion follows that it is necessary for the child to act, for his voice, eyes, and hands to be constantly occupied.

III   *Summary of the Method*

In terms of its own time, Pestalozzi's method was radical. Niederer described the method's aim as follows:

The principle of Pestalozzi when he took over the castle and founded the Institute [at Burgdorf] was revolutionary. By word and deed he wanted to tear down and build up again: tear down the whole school system as it had existed up to then, a system which appeared to him monstrous; then to build up a new school system in which he wanted to entrust the subjects taught to the basic elements and methods of nature. The subjects taught had to be adapted to the nature of the child, to the range of activity of which he was capable, to the stage of his development and to his individual needs. The basic elements of instruction he wished to educe from the physical, mental, moral, and religious nature of the child, from its elemental appearances. The course of instruction had to be brought into complete harmony with the stages of development of human nature.[13]

Henry Holman, author of a standard biography of Pestalozzi, concluded that the general principles of Pestalozzianism could be summarized as follows: (1) education must be essentially religious, since man has a divine origin and end; (2) education must develop man as a whole; (3) education must guide and stimulate self-activity; (4) all education must be based upon intuition and exercise—Pestalozzi's theory of *Anschauung*; (5) education must observe a right graduation and progression in development, for "each child should be taught that which he has to learn at the time his nature calls for it, for this is proof that his sensibility and power are ready for it"; (6) education must foster the growth of knowledge through the development of ideas; from mere vague impressions, the mind must evolve values and meanings.[14]

The foregoing six principles, again according to Holman, form the foundation for certain practical rules which should be involved in the educational process: (1) an all-round training must be given; (2) all possible liberty must be allowed to the learner; (3) work is more important than words, since "man is much more truly educated through that which he does than through that which he learns"; (4) the method of learning must primarily be analytic, that is, based upon the analysis of experience; (5) realities must come before symbolism in education; (6) organization and correlation are necessary—referring to the relations between mind and body, the nature of the child and of knowledge, and the pupil and school conditions.[15]

IV   *Rejection of Books*

In a strong reaction to the superficial book knowledge that had formed the basis of education up to his time, Pestalozzi viewed such learning as an empty mockery. His sentiments are expressed in this statement:

A man who has only word-wisdom is less susceptible to truth than a savage. This use of mere words produces men who believe they have reached the goal, because their whole life has been spent in talking about it, but who never ran toward it, because no motive impelled them to make the effort; hence I come to the conviction that the fundamental error—the blind use of words in matters of instruction—must be extirpated before it is possible to resuscitate life and truth.[16]

On the basis of such declarations, it has frequently been stated that the Pestalozzian method discards the use of books, and relies entirely upon the principle "A child should never be told what he can find out for himself." The charge is refuted by Pestalozzi's associate Hermann Krüsi, who asserted that it was "the *abuse*, and not the *use*, of books which is called in question by the advocates of this system."[17] The Pestalozzian method was based on the idea that children's first lessons in every subject should be presented through the senses; they should examine things, rather than read about them; and what they discover for themselves should be expressed in their own words, rather than adopted from what they find in books. This principle is especially valid in the natural sciences, which can hardly be understood without illustration, direct observation, and experimentation.

After the elements are learned in the various branches, however, books may be used to advantage according to the Pestalozzian belief, if they are subjected to intelligent criticism and not accepted without question. It was recognized that the records of the past are preserved in language and transmitted in books. Thus, books were to be used to supplement experience, and to provide facts not accessible by direct investigation. What Pestalozzi rejected was indirect experience through the printed page rather than direct experience, whenever it was possible to gain the latter. Under traditional schooling, students memorized the literary form of a lesson, often without understanding its meaning. Such a scheme, in Pestalozzi's judgment, did not develop or make use of a child's intelligence.

After the Neuhof experiment, despite Pestalozzi's statement that he "had not read a book for thirty years," he began an extensive program of reading in philosophy, ecclesiastical and constitutional history, and other fields, including works by Shaftesbury, Rousseau, Voltaire, Hume, Mendelssohn, Kant, and Jacobi, as well as contemporary writings and monthly periodicals, extracting what he thought would be relevant for his purpose.

F. H. Hayward, in his *The Educational Ideas of Pestalozzi and Fröbel*, commented: "When Rousseau, Pestalozzi and Fröbel denounce books and bookishness, we must recognize that they are talking nonsense. . . . Rousseau's name is essentially that of a bookwriter, and much of Pestalozzi's best work was of the same kind. . . . Pestalozzi as a teacher did more for the teaching of reading than any other man. The 'bookishness' that followed the Renaissance took wrong forms . . . but it is pernicious and reactionary to talk—as Rousseau and Pestalozzi talked—of making schools less 'bookish.' "

Rousseau, Fröbel, and Pestalozzi were in revolt against the traditions of the Renaissance, as was previously noted. That era had led to the enthronement in all schools of book knowledge. The men of the Renaissance had discovered the treasures of ancient learning and they were so entranced by the discovery —especially as the invention of printing helped to disseminate books—that they set out to transform every school into an institution where the classical languages, and practically nothing else, could be taught. A "scholar" meant a reader of Latin and Greek books. All else was neglected.

V *Student Discipline*

The discipline connected with Pestalozzi's method was naturally mild. Throughout his career he maintained that the school should be as nearly like the home as possible and that the chief incentives to do right are not fear of punishment but kindness and love. In a sympathetic atmosphere, which Pestalozzi always endeavored to provide, with the children engaged in interesting activities and due regard given to their physical, intellectual, and moral needs, severe punishment was seldom required. On this point Pestalozzi remarked: "I do not venture to assert that corporal punishment is inadmissible, but I do object to its application when the teacher or the method is at fault and not the children,"[18] a sentiment strongly echoed a couple of generations later by Horace Mann for the public schools of Massachusetts. The guiding philosophy of noncorporal punishment was adopted by Pestalozzi beginning with his first educational ventures. Concerning his experiences at Stans, for example, he wrote:

When children were persistently obstinate and rude severity was necessary, and I had to use corporal punishment. When conditions are favorable, it is possible to rely altogether on the pedagogical principle which says that we should win the hearts and minds of a crowd of children by words alone; but in a mixture of dissimilar beggar children such as I had to deal with, differing in age and in their deeply-rooted habits, when forced, too, by the needs of the situation to accomplish my aims rapidly, corporal punishment was a necessity, but I did not thereby lose the confidence of my children. . . . My punishments never produced obstinacy in the children, on the contrary they were quite happy if I gave them my hand and kissed them a moment afterwards. . . . I always did my utmost to make them understand clearly the motives of my action in all matters likely to excite their attention or their passions.[19]

In his *Leonard and Gertrude*, Pestalozzi urged that strict order must be observed in the school as preparation for life. School must begin exactly on schedule and no one must be tardy. The children must come clean in person and clothing, and with their hair combed. The body must be kept erect when the child is standing, sitting, writing, or working. Nothing must be thrown upon the floor, children may not eat during lessons, and in rising and sitting down, they must not push against each other. Punishments were made to fit the crime: an idle child had to cut firewood or perform other chores, a forgetful child had to be messenger for several days, disobedient and impertinent children were not spoken to in public for several days, wickedness and lying were punished by the rod. Otherwise, the master treated the children with all kindness and tried to help them overcome their faults.

One important caution offered by Pestalozzi he felt should govern all punishments. The first essential is that a child have a clear idea of what is right and what is wrong. Adults should not assume that the child knows the difference by instinct. To punish an innocent child or one who believes himself innocent will create resentment and loss of trust. In Pestalozzi's canon, discipline should be neither too harsh nor too lenient, but a compromise between the two. As in all other aspects of education, the guiding rule should be the good of the child himself.

Because Pestalozzi had some doubts about the good judgment of his young assistants in administering corporal punishment, he reserved this right for himself.

VI *Preparation of Teachers*

The idea of the professional training of teachers probably originated with Pestalozzi. His ideal teacher was expected to be an expert not only in his subject but also in his knowledge of the child. In Pestalozzi's words: "The schoolmaster should at least be an open-hearted, cheerful, affectionate, and kind man, who would be as a father to the children; a man made on purpose to open children's hearts and their mouths and to draw forth their understandings, as it were, from the hindermost corners. In most schools, however it is just the contrary. The schoolmaster seems as if he were made on purpose to shut up children's mouths and hearts, and then bury their good understandings ever so deep under ground."[20]

The teacher's first duty, Pestalozzi maintained, is to arouse and keep alive the children's interest in study. Almost invariably, any failure on the part of student to apply themselves can be traced to a lack of interest, and that in turn comes from the teacher's mode of teaching. If the teacher neglects to devote his full attention to the subject being taught, makes little effort toward being clearly understood, and does not try to win the affection of his pupils, Pestalozzi believed that he would alienate the children and make them indifferent to his instruction.

Pestalozzi was severely critical of "thousands" of schoolmasters "who have—solely on account of their unfitness to earn a respectable livelihood in any other way—subjected themselves to the laboriousness of this occupation; and they, in accordance with their unsuitability for anything better, look upon their work as leading to nothing further, but sufficient to keep them from starvation."[21]

The obvious conclusion drawn by Pestalozzi was that schoolmastering is not a highly skilled profession, but it is one that demands persons of integrity, understanding, and intelligence. Such individuals are not common. Because teaching is the most important as well as the most difficult profession, those qualified by nature should be sought out and properly trained for their work.

In advocating teacher training, Pestalozzi's chief interest was the preparation of elementary school teachers for rural children, children who often came from poor families. He was less concerned with the matter of preparing teachers for secondary schools, which were attended by children of the upper classes. Morever, Pestalozzi was convinced that the best teachers for the poor come from the ranks of those who themselves have risen from the same social class and background.

Pestalozzi was convinced that a science of education, which could be taught to prospective teachers, might be developed, thereby making teaching a much more effective and efficient process. In a New Year's address in 1818, he declared that on the basis of his own long experience he was confident that "education in all its parts must necessarily be raised to the dignity of a science which must find its foundation in the deepest knowledge of human nature." Pestalozzi added, "I am myself, of course, far from being acquainted with this science. The idea of it is scarcely yet complete in my own mind, yet my mind accepts it as an absolute truth, and the circumstances of the time have made it a necessity for the world." In Pestalozzi's view, "such a science is the most important of all branches of mature knowledge." The effective teacher deliberately makes use of natural forces to attain definite aims.

VII *Mutual Instruction*

From the beginning Pestalozzi believed in the instruction of children by children. In a letter about his Stans experience, he remarks, "Some of my children developed so well that I found that they were able to do some of the work that I did."[22] Elsewhere, in *Leonard and Gertrude*, he writes, in speaking of Gertrude's children, "All that they learned they knew so thoroughly that they were able to teach it to others; and they often asked to teach younger children—this they were allowed to do."[23] While at Stans, Pestalozzi put into practice his theory of mutual instruction, the success of which he afterwards described:

The number and inequality of my children rendered my task easier. Just as in a family the eldest and cleverest child readily shows what he knows to his younger brothers and sisters, and feels proud and happy to be able to take his mother's place for a moment, so my children were delighted when they knew something they could teach others. . . . In this way I soon had helpers and collaborators among the children themselves. . . . Children became the teachers of children."[24]

The fundamental objective of Pestalozzi's educational doctrine was the uplifting of the poor, to improve the miserable state in which they existed. His fame rests upon his reputation as an educator, but his educational theories, especially his views on teacher education, can be understood only in the light of his social philosophy.

CHAPTER 8

Social and Political Reformer

PESTALOZZI was above all else a political and social reformer, and his educational principles were a part of his social philosophy, all directed toward a fervent desire for the betterment of his people and his country. He was past fifty when serfdom was abolished in Switzerland. From his early youth, he found intolerable the conditions which made the peasants of his native country as much in bondage as those of Russia. The mass of the Swiss population was without rights, without material comforts, and even without the necessities of life.

To remedy the miseries of the poor people with whom he was surrounded, Pestalozzi's childhood fancy was first attracted by the example of his uncle and he wanted to follow in the latter's footsteps as a village pastor. But while a student of theology at Zurich, he came under the influence of Rousseau's writings, and, seized by an intense spirit of reform, determined to enter the legal profession in order to be able to defend the people's rights. After abandoning both theology and law, for reasons previously noted, Pestalozzi turned to agriculture, which, according to Rousseau's "back to the soil" movement, could prove the nation's salvation. The orphanage he established on his farm at Neuhof has been described as probably the first industrial school for poor children.

In his earliest writings, Pestalozzi is revealed as an ardent patriot, sharply critical of the existing abuses and inequalities of society—a social order that imposed heavy burdens upon the many poor and conferred its privileges upon the wealthy few. As early as 1792, in his contributions to a Swiss journal, Pestalozzi was dealing with such topics as: "The Temptations which Surround Females of the Lower Classes," "Corruption of Servants in Great Houses," "The Want of Even-Handed Justice Between the Rich and the Poor," "Men With and Without Influence," "The

Hypocrisy of the Privileged Classes and Their Indifference to the Real Suffering of the People," and "The Moral Improvement of Criminals and the Defects of Charity." In these and other articles, Pestalozzi constantly advocates the cause of the poor and oppressed. Throughout his career, he wrote extensively, not only on education, but on politics, finance, jurisprudence, military affairs, industrial questions, and such social problems as infanticide, the home, and the church. A common thread runs through all his literary efforts—the elevation of the poor, the destitute, and the weak.

Despite his denouncements of a corrupt government and a selfish aristocracy, Pestalozzi did not accuse the rulers and lawmakers of bearing the sole responsibility for all social evils. The real source of those evils, he concluded, was to be found in the ignorance and depravity of the population as a whole. There would be no despots, if there were no cringing slaves; no political deceivers, if all the rest were honest; no hypocrites, if simple piety always found its rewards; no quacks and humbugs, if the number of dupes was not so great. More and more, Pestalozzi became convinced that the true remedy for existing political evils was the education of the masses.

Little faith was placed by Pestalozzi in the political process for ameliorating conditions. As one biographer, J. A. Green, noted:

Around him he saw, on the one hand, ignorance, poverty, and degradation; on the other, a crowd of insincere politicians whose rhetoric was empty and inconsequent, because it did not spring from a first-hand acquaintance with facts. Words void of real meaning were bandied about from man to man as if they were true coin. For the moment the position seemed hopeless. Here was wretchedness and misery in plenty, and in the face of it, abundance of talk concerning "the rights of man" and other formulae current at the time, high-sounding, but in their use hollow and unreal. What else could be expected, when education, from top to bottom, dealt with nothing but words, grammatical or ecclesiastical formulae which did not touch in any way the real lives of those who learned them? Education wrongly conceived was the source of much social mischief; education rightly understood and rightly carried out was the only radical cure.[1]

Pestalozzi recognized that the usual efforts toward social betterment seemed to increase rather than reduce the evils at which they were aimed. He observed that philanthropic measures, such as work done by charitable agencies, welfare services, and private philanthropy, no matter how well intentioned, left men more dependent than before. Men were not taught to help themselves. "The best service man can render to man," wrote Pestalozzi, "is to teach him to help himself. Man as a whole in his inner nature must be improved if the external circumstances of the poor are to be bettered."[2] Social reform was likely to come only through proper education of the individual person.

Commenting further on this point, Pestalozzi adds:

If we wish to aid the poor man, the very lowest among the people, we can do so only in one way, namely, by changing the schools of the people into places of true education, in which the moral, mental and physical powers, which God has put into our nature, may be drawn out, so that a man may be enabled to live such a life as he should live happy in himself, and a blessing to others. Only in this way can a man, whom in the whole world nobody does really help because nobody can truly help, learn to help himself.[3]

It was the principle of social progress through education of the poor that Pestalozzi was striving always to make universal in application.

In *Leonard and Gertrude*, Pestalozzi maintained that if men are impoverished in mind and body they become degraded in all respects and naturally fall victims to such deplorable weaknesses as dishonesty, low cunning, craftiness, suspicion, wild violence, revengefulness, and cruelty. They lose all love of mankind, and instead develop the worst animal instincts—cruelty to their own children, treachery to each other, and bestial living. Rather than becoming assets to society, in accordance with the natural potentials they possess, society is faced with the dangers and disasters of having to control viciously disposed human beings.

Purely from mercenary, selfish motives, therefore, society should aim to derive the best from every member of the social body, including the working classes. Even intelligent slave owners, asserted Pestalozzi, realize that the better the workers are cared for the better it will be for their owners. A man's value to the community in which he lives depends upon the full development of his abilities and the proper use of his trained powers. Otherwise, he remains in a primitive state. Education provides the sole machinery for preparing individuals for their rightful place in the community.

Education as viewed by Pestalozzi, however, was no head-in-the-clouds affair. Education must be practical from the point of view of preparing each person to find happiness in his life's work, whatever it may be, and above all to become a useful member of society, even if it is only as a plowman, rat-catcher, or some other lowly occupation. Moreover, every man should be educated for his station in life—lawyer, legislator, clergyman, common laborer, or whatever calling.

In like manner, insisted Pestalozzi, as noted earlier, the poor should be educated for poverty. Children in orphanages, for example, should be thus prepared for life. Some have criticized this concept, but others consider that Pestalozzi was being thoroughly realistic. The critics feel that in advocating an education differentiated according to social class his point of view was too reactionary and was inconsistent with the progressive and enlightened ideas he often stated concerning teaching methods and the learning process. His position is summed up by Pestalozzi in these words:

I simply put to myself the question: What would you do if you wished to give a single child all the theoretical knowledge and practical skill which he requires in order to be able to attend properly to the great concerns of life, and so attain to inward contentment? . . . . What are the means of developing in the child those practical abilities, which the ultimate purpose of his existence, as well as the changeable positions and relations of life, will or may require of him, and cultivating them to such a degree of perfection that the fulfilment of his duties will be to him, not only possible or easy, but in reality a second nature?[4]

A recent commentator, John C. Osgood, concludes that "Pestalozzi was a very competent sociologist, even by modern standards," in defending the doctrine that "the poor person must be educated for poverty." Osgood continues:

In other words, the children of the rural peasantry, most of whom were then living at marginal subsistence levels, must indeed be educated, but they must be educated in such a manner as would enable them to be productive, self-supporting, and self-respecting members of the social class in which the vast majority of them would be destined to remain. Pestalozzi was forced, due of them would be destined to remain. Pestalozzi was forced, due to the exigencies of the social milieu surrounding him and in which he himself was deeply immersed, to think not of the mute, inglorious Miltons but of the fate of the majority. Such was his answer to one of the important and abiding issues of education. Should the emphasis be upon the individual, or should it be upon the class, the society, the aggregate?[5]

Pestalozzi believed that "the poor are poor because they have not been trained to earn their living." But, in addition, he held that all poor children should be "given a profound and accurate knowledge of the needs, restraints and conditions of poverty and also a knowledge of the details of probable conditions of their future lives."[6]

A persuasive argument used by Pestalozzi with governmental officials, as it was later by Horace Mann in dealing with Massachusetts business and industrial leaders, was that education has an important cash value. If children of the poor are provided with vocational education, they will not become burdens on society as adults and the state will be relieved of their future care.

Pestalozzi did not, on the other hand, advocate vocational or industrial training to the exclusion of general education. The earliest education, on the contrary, must be general and preparatory. Special or professional education will then be built upon a well-prepared mind. To omit practical education, however, produces simply preachers and talkers instead of doers and thinkers. The first aim of industrial education is, of course, vocational, but to Pestalozzi it represented something more: "It is the essence of the true art of human education to transform various works and branches of industry into the means of human culture." The cultivation of the laboring man's senses and physical abilities is essential in making "him happy in his positions and relations."[7] Briefly, the Pestalozzian motto was education through and for work. Both Comenius and John Locke had earlier introduced manual work into their proposed curricula for elementary education, but without intending that it should be of much practical use for later life. In fact, Locke had an unrealized plan for establishing a "working school" for the poor, an institution which was to have been simply a combination of a common workshop and a day nursery. To Pestalozzi, therefore, undoubtedly belongs credit for the first definite conception of an industrial education.

I *Political Creed*

Pestalozzi's political activism, as pointed out earlier, began when he was a college student, through his membership in the historical-political association called the Helvetic Society, organized by a group of able young men of Zurich who referred to themselves as "Patriots." The organization was a kind of youth movement designed to raise the nation's moral standards. Pestalozzi's enthusiastic participation in its activities, and especially his writings denouncing corrupt officials, brought him nothing except trouble, a short jail term, a heavy fine, and blacklisting for any type of preferment in government.

Pestalozzi's early years were marked by much political unrest in Switzerland. The focus was the struggle between the citizens of Geneva and its ruling families. Although nominally a republic, the government of the city was in reality an hereditary oligarchy. During the sixteenth century the citizens had united to defend their area from outside attack. For that purpose, power had been delegated to leading families, who had continued to exercise it long after all danger had disappeared. Gradually further powers were assumed and the ruling class began to look upon its privileged position as an hereditary right.

Toward the end of the seventeenth century, the Genevese dared to question the permanent nature of the privileges and to demand a share in the city's government. A concession was made in 1738 when the right to petition the magistracy was granted. The meaningless nature of the concession was revealed in 1762, when the officials condemned Rousseau's *Emile* and *Social Contract* as dangerous to the state and to religion, and then proceeded to reject a petition for the withdrawal of the verdict. In brief, the magistracy's decision was that any petition refused by it was without merit or validity.

The struggle in Geneva was watched with keen concern by the citizens of Zurich. There, too, the town's leaders looked with suspicion upon attempts to subvert existing institutions. This was the prevailing climate of opinion when Pestalozzi and his associates in the Helvetic Society began agitating for social and political reforms. Silber notes that "the country people in the Lake Zurich district, although politically, socially, and economically dependent on the city, had through diligence and efficiency worked their way up in the cotton and weaving industries, and they now demanded political rights corresponding to their economic achievements."⁸ The demand was strongly opposed; not only did the city government refuse to concede the legal rights asked, but even punished the people for demanding them.

Pestalozzi was thoroughly familiar with, and in sympathy with, the country people's pressure for greater democracy in government. He advocated reform of the Zurich constitution to bring it into line with a more liberal policy, and offered to mediate the differences between the city government and the oppressed people. The end result was that the offer was turned down and Pestalozzi was more unpopular in Zurich than ever. He had hoped to bring about reforms in a peaceful manner, but the obstinacy of the city fathers made inevitable the solution of the political issues by violent measures.

The forced changes coincided with the eruption of the French Revolution. As a close neighbor of France, Switzerland could hardly avoid being drawn into the momentous events. The declaration of the Rights of Man which emerged from the Revolution was in exact accord with Pestalozzi's long-held beliefs. He hoped that the equality of the people which had been stubbornly refused by the monarachy would be granted by the new regime. It was natural, therefore, for Pestalozzi to be an ardent supporter of the new order of things inaugurated by the short-lived Swiss Directory (1798-1803), and he warmly welcomed the constitutional changes redressing ancient wrongs and grievances.

Pestalozzi was drawn further toward the ideals of the French Revolution when the National Assembly conferred upon him the title of honorary citizen of France. The honor was all the more gratifying because his own government had consistently neglected and ignored him. Pestalozzi began to refer to France as his "new fatherland." But as the Reign of Terror superseded the original aims of the Revolution, he, along with other European liberal thinkers, was alienated. He still hoped that the forces of liberty would survive the violence, and he was inclined to justify the excesses of the revolutionary power on the basis of the evils inherited from the French monarchy.

In an essay entitled *Yes or No*, written in 1793, Pestalozzi declared that despotism of any kind was certain to ruin Europe and that the survival of governments depended upon their willingness to yield to that "which is reasonable in the demand of the people for liberty."[9] The good of the French Revolution, he concluded, had been undone by the failure of its leaders to control the violence of their passions.

As the nineteenth century opened, the French were masters in Switzerland, the state treasury was empty, the nation had been devastated by war, and the Helvetian Republic was on the point of collapse. France was ready to impose a new constitution on the country. Pestalozzi, as noted, was elected a member of a deputation to visit Paris and to advise Napoleon on the form of a new government. The mission was fruitless, for Napoleon had already decided that it was to his advantage to abolish the central government and to decree the adoption of a federalist constitution. The independence of the nineteen cantons was restored by the Mediation Act of 1803 and the aristocratic conservatives again became the dominant ruling powers.

Thenceforth for a period of years Pestalozzi remained silent on political matters. His educational enterprises were seriously endangered by the fall of the Helvetian Republic, state funds were withdrawn, and powerful enemies were in the ascendancy. Discretion dictated that he avoid political controversy and concentrate attention on his educational designs.

In the beginning, Pestalozzi was optimistic that the Napoleonic regime would achieve wholesome, much-needed political, economic, and social reforms. With the passage of time his contempt for "Bonaparte" grew. In Pestalozzi's view, Napoleon had destroyed the independence of the individual and had delivered education, religion, and social welfare into hands of brute force, all with complete disregard of man's dignity, liberty, and natural rights.

After Napoleon's downfall in 1814, Switzerland was enabled to throw off the enforced Mediation Act and to draft a constitution of its own choosing. Pestalozzi again became an active spokesman for liberal government during the controversies that raged for more than a year about the form of the new constitution.

Actually, Pestalozzi had little faith in the mass of men as protectors of individual freedom. The root cause of this fact, as he conceived it, was a corrupt civilization. The depraved masses must be raised to a higher level of existence through education. In accord with his lifelong creed, Pestalozzi held that the "only remedy" effective in the salvation of a corrupt civilization is the education of every individual in every nation. He held that Europe's only hope for moral, mental, and social salvation was to educate the people to true humanity.

CHAPTER 9

Moral and Religious Teacher

NUMEROUS writers have discussed and criticized, frequently in contradictory fashion, Pestalozzi's views on moral and religious education. The question of whether Pestalozzi himself was a Christian has drawn positive and negative answers. His associate Niederer, who was trained for the ministry, described him as a deeply religious man from the standpoint of emotions and feelings, but as irreligious and antichristian in his intellectual ideas.

As a child of eighteenth-century rationalism, there is little question that Pestalozzi's thought was deeply affected by the Age of Enlightenment and its humanitarian and idealistic concepts. In his *Researches into the Course of Nature in the Development of the Human Race,* he identifies three levels of human development: the natural man, the social man, and the moral man. The natural man—a concept obviously inspired by Rousseau—is a harmless, good-natured being. "Man in this condition," states Pestalozzi, "is a pure child of his instincts which lead him directly and harmlessly to the satisfaction of his sensory desires. So long as this continues we call him an unspoiled natural man, but so soon as he finds difficulty in satisfying his desires, he loses his harmlessness and his natural good nature; he is now *a natural man spoiled.* Just as the whole human race began its development as an innocent child of nature, so the development of each child has this state of innocence as its point of departure."[1]

The natural man, according to Pestalozzi's doctrine, possesses neither religion nor morality. At the time of his birth the child is in exactly the same state, for, like the natural man, "he knows nothing of evil, of pain, of hunger, of care, of mistrust, of feelings of dependence or insecurity. . . . But as soon as the moment of birth is over the purity of the natural man in the child passes away."[2] He demands immediate satisfaction for his physical wants—an indication of future struggles and pain which will corrupt the pristine state to which he is born.

The spoiled natural man is in many respects a pathetic creature. Selfishness has replaced natural kindliness, and his life becomes a continual battle. He is against every other man and other men's hands are turned against him. Such religion as he possesses is mere superstition. Gradually, over a long period of time, according to eighteenth-century social theory, society and law develop, to provide for the protection of the individual. Social man, however, is not necessarily moral. His actions are regulated by law for the benefit of society, but legality, Pestalozzi insisted, has nothing to do with the religion of true morality.

Most men, according to the Pestalozzian thesis, are content to live their lives under law. Their behavior conforms to all legal requirements, they act the part of good citizens, and socially they are approved by their fellowmen. Morality, on the other hand, is an individual matter. The difference between legality and morality is the difference between necessity and freedom.

Pestalozzi recognized that perfect morality is an unattainable ideal. Mankind is as incapable of living upon earth "a life of pure morality as of remaining in the innocence of his original nature."[3] Indeed, few men even attempt to reach such an ideal. The pressures of society and native selfishness are too strong for them to aspire to moral perfection. Nevertheless, there is in every man a higher nature, a divine element opposed to the selfishness of the spoiled animal nature. A lifelong struggle goes on between these two sides of man. The problem of moral and religious education, Pestalozzi held, is to work for the predominance of the higher nature.

During his lifetime it was often charged that Pestalozzi gave no religious instruction in the various schools with which he was associated. Extensive evidence exists to the contrary. Writing of the moral education of the children at Stans, for example, Pestalozzi observed: "My one aim was to make their new life in common, and their new powers, awaken a feeling of brotherhood amongst the children, and make them affectionate, just and considerate. I reached this end without much difficulty. Amongst these seventy wild beggar-children there soon existed such peace, friendship and cordial relations as are rare even between actual brothers and sisters."[4]

To the orthodox, Pestalozzi's cardinal sin was his neglect of, and even strong opposition to, two practices that were universal in his time. He felt that to make the Bible the child's first reader was fundamentally wrong. He was equally certain that to make a child learn the catechism by heart could produce only evil results. "Catechism about abstract ideas," he comments, "excepting the advantage of separating words and subjects into analytic forms, is nothing in itself but a parrot-like repetition of unintelligible sounds." He adds, "I have been bold to say before now that God hates stupidity, hypocrisy and lip-service, and that we should teach children to think, feel and act rightly, and lead them to enjoy the blessings of faith and love that are natural to them, before we make them commit various points of dogma and theological controversy to memory as an intellectual and spiritual exercise."[5] The downgrading of the catechism was the main source of criticism among those inclined to condemn Pestalozzi's methods.

On the other side, surviving accounts from several former pupils refer to the fact that every morning before breakfast Pestalozzi delivered a discourse, sometimes based on a Scriptural text, sometimes on a verse from some familiar hymn, sometimes on a moral duty. He also gave moral guidance to individuals and to small groups. Further, there were prayers at the beginning and end of the day, and every Friday the story of the Passion was read.

In Pestalozzi's view, his curriculum in its entirety was religious, because it was based on the cultivation of both heart and mind, one directed to love and the other to truth; love and truth, it was maintained, are simply two different names for God. To refute the charges of opponents that his method was predominantly intellectual, neglected moral education, and was contrary to the Christian faith, Pestalozzi insisted upon the primary need for training of the mind, for through intellectual education the moral powers of effort, self-control, and independent decision are cultivated as well. "As for moral education as a separate study," Silber points out, "it is difficult to formulate laws and to establish results. If morality is put into words, there is always the danger of achieving its opposite, mere prattle and sheer hypocrisy."[6]

The most frequently cited account of Pestalozzi's views on religious education is to be found in the closing chapters of his

work *How Gertrude Teaches Her Children*. At the outset, the
question is raised, "How is it that the conception of God origi-
nates in my mind? How do I come to believe in Him, to trust
Him and to love Him?" The answer is, "I soon see that the feelings of love, trust, gratitude and readiness to obey, must be developed in me before I can apply them to God. I must love men,
trust men, thank men, and obey men before I can aspire to love,
thank, trust and obey God."[7]

From this premise naturally arises another question: how does
one learn to love his fellowmen? "All love," concludes Pestalozzi,
"arises from the relationship that exists between the infant and
his mother."[8] He insists that family life is the true source of religion and morality. Continuing the same theme, Pestalozzi holds
that the child's earliest experiences in his relations with his
mother are the main sources of "inner feelings," a determining
factor in his moral and religious future. The germs of love, of
trust, and of gratitude are developed in the child through perfect
intimacy and understanding with his mother. As phrased by Pestalozzi:

The development of the human race begins in a strong passionate desire
for the satisfaction of physical wants. The mother's breast satisfies the
physical cravings, and generates *love*; soon after, *fear* is developed, but
the mother's protecting arm drives it away and the child *trusts*. Love and
trust united produce the first germ of gratitude . . . . It is in the stimulation of these first physical manifestations of trust and love that the first
physical manifestations of morality and religious feeling spring and develop.

The child's gradual progression from the simple satisfaction of
physical desires to feelings of trust, love, and gratitude for his
mother is largely instinctive or intuitive. He does not think or
reason, he merely feels. Real love and trust come later. In the
same way, the child learns to be patient and obedient. He discovers he must share his mother's attention with others, that he
does not have exclusive call upon her time. He sees her caress
other children, from which are born the germs of social feelings,
sympathy, and brotherly love—the first principles of moral self-
development.

As the child develops physically, he is inclined to be more and
more independent of his mother. "He becomes conscious of his
own personality and secretly begins to feel that he no longer

needs his mother."[10] According to Pestalozzi, the mother must expect, sympathize with, and help her child to gain independence of herself. In his *On Infants' Education* he writes:

In the progress of time the child not only is daily exercising and strengthening its physical faculties, but it begins also to feel intellectually and morally independent. From observation and memory there is only one step to reflection. Though imperfect, yet this operation is frequently found among the early exercises of the infant mind. . . . The child, then begins to judge for himself, not of things only, but also of men: he acquires an idea of character: he grows, more and more, *morally independent.*[11]

Thus, Pestalozzi identifies several stages in a child's moral development. In the first period of the child's life, he is guided only by feeling and intuition; the mother is the center of his world. In the second stage, the child's love, trust, and obedience extend to a wider circle, he begins to use words, to talk, to use his hands, to walk. Then a time arrives when he no longer feels completely dependent upon his mother, as he mingles with other children and learns to trust his own abilities. This is seen by Pestalozzi as a critical time. Either the child ceases to trust, to obey, and to love his mother and becomes rebellious, selfish, and overselfconfident, or the instinctive feelings of love, gratitude, and obedience which have been centered on his mother are transferred to mankind and to higher morality and religion. The conflict between good and evil takes place in the child's world, that is, in the home, where love, trust, gratitude, unselfishness, and service are developed, where the head, heart, and hand are trained under the mother's guidance. Much depends upon the mother, for she herself must be moral and possess qualities of the divine in her nature in order to impart true morality to her child.

The foundation of morality, Pestalozzi maintains, is love. Love he calls the original power, the beginning and end of human development, the most basic emotion, the divine spark which differentiates man from beast. Without love, intellectual education is sterile and ineffective. The connecting link between moral and intellectual education is love. True to his theory that all knowledge comes through language, form, and number, Pestalozzi uses language as a device for moral education. Truth, he concludes, is arrived at through language, which he calls "the gift which makes man truly human," for by way of language man's feelings are communicated, personal relationships are established, and a medium is provided for expressing love.

The preschool period was seen by Pestalozzi as vitally significant in the child's moral and religious growth. By the time a child arrives in school he should have developed a trust in God, a belief in human virtues, and a desire to serve his fellowmen. In effect, the most important years of his life as far as moral education is concerned are over. Ideally, the best means for continuance of moral training is a well-regulated family life, such as Pestalozzi pictured in Leonard and Gertrude's household. And here the poor are likely to have an advantage over the rich, for their family life offers many opportunities for mutual helpfulness, self-sacrifice, and loving sympathy.

No school can take the place of a happy, well-adjusted family, in Pestalozzi's judgment, because the intellectual, moral, and physical forces at work in the home are the most intimate, natural, and educational in nature. Nevertheless, the school can accomplish much, if its efforts are properly directed. The school is equipped beyond the ability of the family to carry on the educational process. As far as possible, the transition from home to school ought to be easy and natural. The school should aim at continuing family life and at creating an atmosphere closely resembling the family. In dealing with his pupils, the teacher should accept as a model the relation between parent and children. Pestalozzi noted that his first efforts at Stans were directed toward making the seventy children feel like brothers and sisters in a large family, to encourage mutual affection and consideration for each other.

Whether or not Pestalozzi was a Christian in an orthodox sense may be debatable. In his writings on the subject, he equates pure Christianity with basic morality. Whatever the conclusion, it is certain that Pestalozzi disregarded all forms of Christian dogma. No one, however, can deny the ethical character of his life and work. His attitude toward religion may be traced, at least to a large extent, to his revolt against the educational system of his time. Ignorant schoolmasters, typical of the era, were extremely bigoted and conservative in dealing with all religious matters. Their theological views, even though little comprehended, were rigidly orthodox and stubbornly held—legacies of the long, bitter struggle between Catholic and Protestant factions. Too, Pestalozzi adhered strongly to the belief that abstract ethical and theological systems should be left to mature minds. A child must experience and live religion before he is taught *about* religion. Theology, in its theoretical aspects, no matter how simplified for the child's mind, should come after religious experience. In short, the basis of moral education is practice rather than preaching.

As early as the Stans experiment, Pestalozzi reports that he taught the children "neither morality nor religion" and attempted few explorations of moral principles. Instead, his aim was to establish through example, and by arousing feelings of love, confidence, and sympathy, a sense of right and wrong. At Yverdon also, Pestalozzi's efforts were directed toward making the environment, not formal religious instruction, the chief factor in the moral education of his pupils. In his *Report to Parents* (1808), he holds that formal educational organization is of value only to the extent that it succeeds in emulating and reproducing the home environment, by which Pestalozzi meant a proper religious atmosphere, such as he described in *Leonard and Gertrude*. During an interview at Yverdon in 1816, Pestalozzi, speaking of ways of stimulating the child to do his best work, remarked that "he never appealed to all-too-easily excited motives like that of love of praise. The children were expected to respond to purer ones, such, for example, as love of duty, of parents, of teachers, and above all love for the subject itself, to which the child must be won by such a treatment of the subject as corresponded to his intellectual standpoint."[12]

Pestalozzi saw only harmony, and no conflict, between Christianity and his teaching of morals. Education according to nature, his method, was meant to control man's animal nature and to develop and to encourage his spiritual nature. "In the spirit of Jesus Christ," Pestalozzi declares, "elementary education teaches the child to strive for the highest and best of which his nature is capable."[13] Thus, there was no fundamental difference in Pestalozzi's eyes between the elementary method devised by him and the teachings of Jesus.

An examination of Pestalozzi's voluminous writings makes clear that he regarded moral education as the key to his whole structure. Intellectual, practical, and moral education should be inseparable, and of these, moral education is the capstone. "My morality," concludes Pestalozzi, "is nothing else than the way in which I apply my pure will to do right, to the measure of my knowledge and to the concrete circumstances of my life."[14]

CHAPTER 10

European Influence

F ROM the early stages on, Pestalozzi's ideas and the result of his experiments passed the boundaries of Switzerland.

Not surprisingly, perhaps, his homeland was relatively slow in following Pestalozzi's lead, bearing out the axiom "A prophet is not without honor save in his own country." Various factors contributed to this state of affairs. Different languages spoken in the several cantons were divisive, hampering the exchange of ideas. The inhabitants of the Catholic cantons were under bigoted ecclesiastical control, which frowned upon progress or change of any sort. Even in the Protestant cantons, the people of the rural areas and of the old city corporations were so steeped in conservatism that they viewed with suspicion all efforts to alter their timeworn customs and institutions.

Thus, while the schools founded by Pestalozzi at Burgdorf and Yverdon were receiving enthusiastic students and visitors from all parts of Europe, the national, cantonal, and local governments of Switzerland were slow to incorporate the new concepts of education into their systems of teaching. An exception was Zurich, the only truly progressive city in the Alps. Previously, Zurich had given birth and substantial aid to the great religious reformer Zwingli and to the philosopher Johann Caspar Lavater. Now it welcomed and supported the principles being developed by Pestalozzi. Here Karl August Zeller of Würtemberg, who had visited Burgdorf and witnessed the work in progress, gave a series of lectures, largely attended by teachers and clergymen, to aid in the establishment of a teachers' seminary based upon Pestalozzian principles. Hermann Krüsi, after leaving the Yverdon institute, founded a number of schools and carried Pestalozzianism into various parts of Switzerland, and also contributed extensively to Pestalozzian literature. Also of wide influence were the activities of Emanuel von Fellenberg, Pestalozzi's friend and disciple, who established several industrial and agricultural schools to advance agriculture and to improve Swiss education through training the children of the poor. The marked success of the Fellenberg institutions led to the establishment of similar schools in other countries.

I *Germany*

The most profound impact of Pestalozzi's methods, however, was felt not in his native land but in Germany. Furthermore, it was chiefly through Germany, rather than directly from Switzerland, that Pestalozzi's ideas spread to other countries. Young Germans were sent to Switzerland to study at Burgdorf and Yverdon and returned home full of enthusiasm for the new movement. Pestalozzi's *Leonard and Gertrude* deeply impressed Queen Louisa of Prussia, who wrote: "I am now reading Leonard and Gertrude by Pestalozzi. How refreshing this story of the Swiss village is! Were I my own master, I would go straightway to Switzerland to shake hands with the noble man, and to thank him with all my heart. How deep is his love for his fellow men. Yes, in the name of humanity, I thank him."[1]

After the disastrous and humiliating defeat of the Prussian army by Napoleon's forces at Jena in 1806, Germany for several years thereafter was under the nearly absolute domination of the French emperor. Only civil and municipal affairs were left in the hands of local authorities. During the dreary period of subjugation, political apathy, and despair, the ablest German philosophers and statesmen were seeking means to raise the physical, mental, and moral character of their fellow countrymen and to bring about national regeneration.

The vital spark appears to have been provided by Johann Gottlieb Fichte in his rousing addresses to the German people on behalf of national education under the Pestalozzian system. While a private tutor at Zurich from 1789 to 1792, Fichte had become acquainted with the educational views of Pestalozzi. Outstanding courage was required to advocate a comprehensive system of popular and liberal education in the midst of foreign military occupation of the country's fortresses and cities. Nevertheless, Fichte combined a patriot's enthusiasm and a prophet's inspiration to picture a system of public education—subsequently adopted by Prussia—which he was convinced would achieve the moral, spiritual, and mental reform of his fellow Germans. The Fichte addresses were fourteen in number. After speaking of the general principles of the new education he proposed, Fichte devoted several lectures to the question of the national characteristics of the German people. In the tenth and later addresses he comes to a more definite treatment of the details of the educational program he was advancing. Concerning Pestalozzi's system, Fichte comments:

Pestalozzi must needs remain in the history of our age one of the most extraordinary and beautiful phenomena. This his contemporaries feel; posterity will appreciate it still more deeply. To the course of instruction which has been invented and brought forward by Heinrich Pestalozzi, and which is now being successfully carried out under his direction —must we look for our regeneration. . . . With this system of popular education for the entire rising generation must the nation address itself—at once and persistently.[2]

Prior to Fichte's landmark lectures, by the beginning of the nineteenth century Pestalozzianism had begun to find its way into Prussia. Pestalozzi's appeal, in 1801, for a public subscription to support the Burgdorf institute was generously supported. The next year, Herbart's book *Pestalozzi's ABC of Observation* attracted a vast deal of attention. In 1803, a representative was sent from Prussia to Burgdorf to report upon the new system. Other Pestalozzian missionaries were rapidly making converts. Johann Ernst Plamann, who had visited Burgdorf, established a Pestalozzian school in Berlin in 1805, and published several texts applying the new methods to language, geography, and natural history. During the same year, Anton Grüner opened at Frankfort a similar school, which was later to start Friedrich Fröbel upon an educational career. Christian Heinrich Zeller was brought from Würtemberg to lecture to large audiences at the Königsberg seminary, and while there organized a Pestalozzian orphanage. An institution of the same type for educating orphans was established at Potsdam by Wilhelm von Turk.

In his zeal for public education, Fichte was ardently supported by King Friedrich Wilhelm III and Queen Louisa, who felt that only through the advanced educational principles proposed by him could a restoration be achieved of the territory and prestige lost to Napoleon at Jena. At the same time, Prussia was fortunate in its ministers, von Stein and von Humboldt, who successively guided her educational policies in full accord with Pestalozzi's ideas. Teachers sent to Switzerland for training and observation were placed in positions of responsibility upon their return home. Minister of Education Süvern addressed a group of twelve young men immediately before their departure for Yverdon in these words:

The object in sending you to Pestalozzi is, not merely that you may study the external or formal part of this system, or to acquire skill in teaching, but that you may warm yourselves at the sacred fire which is glowing in the bosom of that man, who is full of power and love; that you may walk with a similar spirit in the path of truth and in the observation of the laws of nature; that you may become simple as children, in order to obtain the key with which to open the sacred temple of childhood; that you may never forget, that a knowledge of the elementary part of each science is the most difficult to obtain, since it requires a thorough perception of the reality of things; that the characteristic feature of the Pestalozzian method is the fact of its being equally adapted for scientific research and for popular application, since it does not spoil the desire for knowledge by light and unwholesome food, but strengthens it by vigorous nourishment.[3]

In response to a request from Pestalozzi for an audience with him to present his educational philosophy, Napoleon had replied, "I have no time to occupy myself with the ABC," but by adopting the Pestalozzian principles the German schools were speedily organized upon a new basis and became the most progressive in Europe. The introduction of Pestalozzian ideas into the Prussian schools occurred from approximately 1812 to 1825, at the end of which time they had substantially taken possession of the whole common school system. In the judgment of contemporary German educators, the most important benefits deriving from the change were the following: patriotic feeling, causing more thorough study of the German language, home geography, etc.; the giving of a high value and place to vocal music as a study; the introduction of thorough musical instruction; the emphasis on the value of drawing; and the introduction of a comprehensive system of bodily training. The new scheme of things replaced the reading, singing, and memorizing of texts, songs, and catechism, under the direction of incompetent teachers, characteristic of the past, and also eliminated the unsanitary buildings and brutal punishment of pupils that had formerly prevailed.

By a cabinet order in 1809, the Prussian Minister of Education, von Stein, stated the fundamental principles to be followed in the reorganization of primary instruction: first, education was henceforth to be considered the state's responsibility; second, schoolteachers must prepare themselves for their profession; third, the aim of primary schools was not to impart knowledge but to help form judgment, common sense, morality, and religious spirit; and, fourth, special attention must be paid to the exterior and interior of school buildings, to the cleanliness and sanitary condition of the schoolrooms, and to the pupils' regular attendance.

One of the most active propagators of Pestalozzi's doctrines in Germany was the philosopher and educator Johann Friedrich Herbart. From the beginning, Herbart was attracted by Pestalozzi's ideas on sense perception and on the natural method of teaching. Building upon this basis, Herbart developed what became known in Germany as scientific pedagogy. "The whole field of actual and possible sense-perception is open to the Pestalozzian method," wrote Herbart; "its peculiar merit consists in having laid hold more boldly and more zealously than any former method of the duty of building up the child's mind; of constructing in it a definite experience in the light of clear sense-perception; not acting as if the child had already an experience, but taking care that it gets one."[4] The social implications of Pestalozzi's teachings were also fully realized by Herbart, who stated, "The welfare of the people is Pestalozzi's aim—the welfare of the common, crude population. He desired to take care of those of whom fewest do take care. He did not seek the crown of merit in your mansions, but in your hovels."[5]

Herbart's views were fully endorsed in a statement from Fichte: "Pestalozzi's essential aim has been to raise the lower classes and clear away all differences between them and the educated classes. It is not only popular education that is thus realized, but national education. Pestalozzi's system is powerful enough to help nations, and the whole human race, to rise from the miserable state in which they have been wallowing."[6]

It has been suggested that the elaborate system built by the German philosophers upon Pestalozzi's relatively simple ideas would have been recognized with difficulty by Pestalozzi. Nevertheless, as Green points out, "Herbart, with a new philosophy and a definite ethical system, was able to give the vague intuitions of Pestalozzi a more definite form, to organize them into a system capable of practical interpretation free from the one-sidedness and mechanism into which Pestalozzi himself was often led through the absence of fixed guiding principles."[7]

Among the visitors to Yverdon during its most brilliant period was another German educator, Friedrich Fröbel, who spent more than a year with Pestalozzi and became deeply influenced by the latter's teachings. Fröbel, generally regarded as the founder of the kindergarten system, was the organizer of a number of schools. In his later years, he devoted himself exclusively to the study of preschool children, devised series of educational games and employments for children, established training courses for kindergarten teachers, and introduced kindergartens throughout Germany. Both Fröbel and Pestalozzi believed that education cannot create intelligence, but should be designed to develop the child's inborn faculties or abilities. Both were convinced that the faculties are developed by use, and Fröebel held that such activity should be voluntary, the teacher's chief role being to arouse the child's interest. One of Fröbel's most important works, *The Education of Man* (1826), is throughout reminiscent of Pestalozzi's philosophy, and his motto, "Come, let us live with our children," is a direct reflection of what he had observed and experienced at Yverdon.

Among other eminent educators who introduced Pestalozzianism into Germany, the name of von Turk ranks high. At an early age, von Turk was appointed a judge in Potsdam. After a period of years on the bench, he became increasingly distressed by the many criminal cases brought before him that could be clearly attributed to the early neglect of education. While holding the office of judge, von Turk was appointed school inspector; in that capacity he decided that the teaching vocation, which saves from crime, is more honorable than that of the magistrate, whose duty it is to avenge crime. According to an account by Horace Mann, who visited von Turk in the 1840's, "He immediately resigned his office of judge, with its life tenure and salary; traveled to Switzerland, where he placed himself under the care of Pestalozzi; and after availing himself for three years of the instruction of that celebrated teacher, he returned to take charge of an Orphan Asylum [at Potsdam]. Since that time he has devoted his whole life to the care of the neglected and destitute. . . . Even now . . . he employs himself in teaching agriculture, together with the branches commonly taught in Prussian schools, to a class of orphan boys."[8]

II *France*

A common language had aided in spreading Pestalozzi's doctrines in Germany. Such a favorable factor was lacking in France, Spain, England, and other areas where the dissemination of these ideas proceeded at a slower pace. At the time that Pestalozzi was developing his system, the military spirit in France overshadowed everything else. A despotic rule controlled the people's every activity and there was general apathy toward education at all levels. After the overthrow of Napoleon, France was left in an exhausted and impoverished state. Her primary schools were placed under ecclesiastical control and management—forces predominantly hostile to fresh ideas and to educational innovation.

Despite handicaps, some evidence exists to show that Pestalozzianism had begun to penetrate France at an early date. General Marc Antoine Jullien, a companion of Napoleon's in the Egyptian campaign and an officer of the Legion of Honor, came to Yverdon and spent eight to ten hours daily for several months studying the application of Pestalozzi's methods. Jullien's conclusions were presented to the French public in two works: *Report on the Yverdon Institute in Switzerland* (1810) and *Spirit of Pestalozzi's Educational Method* (1812). The latter work received wide circulation in European countries and was long considered the best contemporary description of the Pestalozzian method. Through the influence of these reports, thirty students were sent from France to Yverdon. It is probable that the establishment of the first French normal school at Strasbourg in 1810 was another result.

Even earlier, in 1805, Chavannes had published a treatise on Pestalozzi's principles. Three years later, the philosopher Maine de Biran had founded a Pestalozzian school which continued until about 1881. Not until after the end of Charles X's despotic rule in 1830, however, did Pestalozzi's ideas have any considerable effect upon French education. The change came with the appointment of Victor Cousins as Minister of Education. Cousins made himself acquainted with the best school systems in Europe, including an extensive examination of the Prussian schools. His associate, Georges Cuvier, at the same time visited schools in Holland, which had been organized substantially upon Pestalozzian principles. The German schools were found by Cousins to be so superior to those of France that he recommended a reconstruction on German models. His conclusions were contained in a highly influential document issued in 1835, *Report on the State of Public Instruction in Prussia,* which proclaimed the great merits of Pestalozzianism in the elementary schools of that country. Cousins's report ends with a semi-apology for proposing adoption of the school system of a rival nation: "The experience of Germany, and particularly of Prussia, ought not to be lost upon us. National rivalries or antipathies would here be completely out of place. The true greatness of a people does not consist in borrowing nothing from others; but in borrowing from all whatever is good, and in perfecting whatever it appropriates."[9]

Cousin's successor as Minister of Education, Francois Guizot, followed the former's lead in urging acceptance of the Prussian schools as the best type for the reform movement, and also for the training of teachers in accord with Pestalozzi's ideals.

III *Spain*

At first, Spain took a favorable view of the Swiss developments, despite the fact that she was one of the least advanced nations of Europe from the standpoint of education. In 1806, the Yverdon institute received from Spain a number of students sent by the government upon direction of King Charles IV, influenced by his favorite, Manuel de Godoy, "Prince of Peace." Voitel of Soleure, a Swiss captain in the Spanish service, began a Pestalozzi-type school in 1805 for a Tarragona regiment, and later organized a normal school at Santander for training teachers in the new method. Finally, in Madrid a special school was established under the name of the Royal Pestalozzian Military Institute. Political events, however, forced an abrupt end to these experiments; the Madrid school was closed in 1808, and education in Spain was surrendered back into the hands of the Jesuits and ecclesiastics. Krüsi, writing some years later, noted that "the nation so far relapsed into barbarism that not one-tenth of the inhabitants could read or write."[10]

IV *Britain*

Pestalozzi received a number of English visitors at Yverdon, among them Robert Owen, the famous philanthropist and social reformer, and Henry Brougham, champion of popular education. A visitor with whom Pestalozzi formed a close friendship was a rather obscure young Englishman, James Pierrepont Greaves. According to an early Pestalozzi biographer, von Raumer, "An Englishman of the name of Greaves visited Yverdon in 1819 [actually 1817]; he offered to teach these poor Swiss children English without remuneration, and his offer was accepted."[11] Another Pestalozzi associate, Vulliemin, wrote that Greaves carried the ideas he had gathered back to England, "where they took root, and became the origin of infant schools." Pestalozzi valued Greaves highly enough to declare that "he of all men most completely understood the end which I had in view."[12] Upon his return to England, Greaves corresponded with Pestalozzi between 1818 and 1820. The Pestalozzi letters were translated and published in English under the title *Letters on Early Education Addressed to J. P. Greaves, Esq. by Pestalozzi* (London, 1827). The original German manuscript has been lost.

In some respects, the letters to Greaves are the fullest exposition available in his own words of Pestalozzi's views, especially on the subject of infant education and the direction of mothers in the training of their children. The *Letters* insisted that a pupil should not be a passive instrument but must be an active agent in his own education.

Another great admirer of Pestalozzi was John Synge, the "Irish Traveller," who visited in Switzerland for several months in 1814, in the course of a European tour. During an extended stopover in Yverdon, Synge familiarized himself with the new principles of teaching. In the preface to his *Biographical Sketch of the Struggles of Pestalozzi*, he related his reactions upon entering a Pestalozzi classroom: "The intelligent countenances of the children and the energetic interest which they appeared to take in their studies forcibly attracted his attention, although the lesson was in German with which he was, at that time, quite unacquainted." Synge concluded that Pestalozzi's principles were applicable to every branch of knowledge and suitable for all ranks of society. Particularly praiseworthy in Synge's eyes was "the removal of all that misery and compulsion which, till now, has clouded the acquirements of our juvenile years."[13]

Upon his return home to Ireland in 1815, Synge opened a school for the village children and set up a printing press to publish a number of anonymous tracts on Pestalozzi's method and masses of materials suitable for teaching the principles. A series of letters were exchanged between Synge and Pestalozzi from 1816 to 1818. Therein Synge reported that his poor-school was flourishing; for three or four hours daily the children were taught language, number, and form and read the Bible. The remainder of their time was spent working on the land, and making footwear and straw hats. Also, some mothers had started to participate in the education of their children, following in Gertrude's footsteps.

The keen interest shown by Greaves, Synge, and other visitors from Britain, and the practical application of his principles in English and Irish schools, persuaded Pestalozzi that the prospects for success might be brightest in that country. "There is no doubt," he wrote, in a letter to a minister of the Czar of Russia in 1818, "that this nation is more advanced and more established in the basic essentials of industry than any other on the Continent. . . . They have entered with rare insight into the main idea that it is necessary to simplify the beginnings of popular education and to restrict it to the essentials so as to give these to the people with solidity and in harmony with their needs."[14]

Best known and most influential of Pestalozzi's English disciples was Dr. Charles Mayo, a clergyman. Mayo, then headmaster of Bridgenorth Grammar School, was inspired by John Synge to give up his post and travel to Yverdon, in 1819, taking with him a number of students. For nearly three years, Mayo remained with Pestalozzi, for whom his affection and appreciation grew steadily. In a letter written home, Mayo comments on the impression made by Pestalozzi: "Every action of his life is characterized by the most exuberant philanthropy. Had it been checked by a little more prudence, it would perhaps have produced more benefit to mankind."[15]

Shortly after his return to England, Mayo started a school for boys from the upper classes in which the teaching was done according to Pestalozzian principles. So successful was the enterprise that within a few years it had to be moved into larger quarters. In addition to operating a school, Mayo gave public lectures on the life of Pestalozzi and supported the teachers' training institution that the Home and Colonial School Society had established. Mayo's sister Elizabeth was also a convert to Pestalozzi's method and assisted her brother in teaching and administration; Elizabeth was the author of a chapter, "Pestalozzi and His Principles," in one of Charles Mayo's books. Whether the Mayos preached the pure gospel, however, is a subject of controversy. A negative point of view is expressed by various commentators, including Gerald Lee Gutek, a recent biographer, who states, "Unfortunately the English Pestalozzians, under the influence of Charles and Elizabeth Mayo, lost sight of the cultivation of the love environment of the general method. . . . In losing sight of the general method the Mayos' version emphasized only one phase of Pestalozzianism, the object lesson." Gutek points out that when Pestalozzi held that sense impression is the source of all ideas, "he did not intend that his principles of natural education should be so distorted as to become a mechanical, rote, catechetical affair in which students replied to a number of previously set questions. The formal object lesson became a corruption of Pestalozzi's theory."[16]

As a matter of fact, in the judgment of Kate Silber, Pestalozzi's foremost modern biographer, "Pestalozzianism was brought to England at an unpropitious time; it came, from one point of view, too early, for interest in popular education had just begun and was still bound up with religious education, and from another, too late, for Pestalozzi himself was too old to exert a strong personal influence, and his institute had lost its international reputation."[17] For these reasons, the impact of Pestalozzianism on English education as a whole was less pronounced than it was on education on the Continent and in America. Only in Germany was the true Pestalozzi spirit absorbed in its entirety. It was through the German example, systematized and well organized, therefore, that Pestalozzi's teachings were eventually transmitted to England, France, and the United States.

CHAPTER 11

Transatlantic Impact

THE Pestalozzi movement reached the United States early in the nineteenth century. The first American disciple appears to have been William Maclure, who was born a Scotsman, but became an American citizen shortly after the Revolutionary War. Maclure was an extraordinarily successful businessman who retired at an early age to devote his energies, time and wealth to scientific and educational work. One of his primary interests was geology, and he spent several years traveling in Europe to study the geology and natural history of the continent and to collect museum specimens. Following his return to America, Maclure prepared the first comprehensive geological map and survey of the United States.

In the course of his European mission, in 1805 Maclure visited Pestalozzi's school at Yverdon. Enthusiastic over what he heard and observed, Maclure attempted to persuade Pestalozzi to emigrate to Philadelphia for the purpose of establishing a new school which Maclure offered to finance. The effort was unsuccessful, but on Pestalozzi's recommendation his former assistant, Joseph Neef, then conducting a Pestalozzian school in Paris, was appointed. Neef emigrated to the new world in 1806 to set up the first Pestalozzian school in America, at Philadelphia.

The Philadelphia school was located on a hill near the Falls of Schuylkill and initially attracted an enrollment of about one hundred boys, mainly from the nearby area. Languages, mathematics, and natural sciences were taught. Neef's methods closely emulated Pestalozzi's. He abolished books from the lower grades and gave instruction orally with the help of blackboards. Nature and geography were taught by field lessons. Music and gymnastics also occupied important places in the educational scheme. Any necessary discipline was administered by student government.

To help popularize Pestalozzianism in the United States, Neef produced and published two works: *Sketch of a Plan and Method of Education*, in 1808, reputed to be the first strictly pedagogical book in the English language; and *The Method of Instructing Children Rationally in the Arts of Writing and Reading*, in 1813. Neef's grasp of Pestalozzi's theories is demonstrated by a statement in the *Sketch*: "Pestalozzi's pupil always sets out from the known and plain, and proceeds with slow speediness to the yet unknown and complicated. He leaves no point behind him without being perfectly master of it. Every point of knowledge which he acquires is but a step to acquire a new one. All his faculties are displayed; but none is overstrained. All his proceedings are subject to the minutest gradation."[1]

The Philadelphia school prospered, but after three years was moved to Village Green in Delaware County, Pennsylvania, presumably for a healthier, more wholesome outdoor life. The number of students decreased and support for the institution gradually declined, in part becase of Neef's reportedly too liberal views on religion. A second move, to Louisville, Kentucky, was even less successful. Neef resigned and the school closed. Neef's failures have been attributed to his imperfect knowledge of English, his lack of understanding of the American character, his inability to adapt Pestalozzian methods to new world conditions, and his too-frequent migrations.

In 1825, however, Maclure recalled Neef to undertake another educational endeavor, to take charge of a Pestalozzian school in the utopian community established by Robert Owen and William Maclure in southern Indiana. Maclure's intention was to make the New Harmony community there the center of American education through introduction of the Pestalozzian system of instruction. Maclure also contemplated the establishment of an industrial school in New Harmony after the manner of Pestalozzi, commenting that "in thus joining mental with corporeal labor, the Pestalozzian system has a great advantage in all schools of industry; for it not only produces both knowledge and property at the same time, but gives habits of working and thinking conjointly, which last during life, and doubles the powers of production, while it alleviates the fatigue of labor by a more agreeable occupation of the mind."[2]

The community experiment in New Harmony collapsed after

only two years, because of dissension between Maclure and Owen, though the School of Industry was carried on independently for several additional years, and a scientific program lasted until the 1840's.

Neither the Philadelphia school nor the New Harmony experiment exerted wide influence on American education. In fact, there was little general adoption of Pestalozzian methods in American schools prior to 1860. Nevertheless, much information about their use in European schools began to permeate the country through articles in American educational and other journals and newspapers during the first half of the century. Returned travelers, such as Calvin Stowe, John Griscom, William C. Woodbridge (editor of *Annals of Education*), and Charles Brooks, published reports on their visits and experiences abroad and proposed adoption of the new principles as a remedy for American educational deficiencies. Griscom's account, entitled *A Year in Europe*, of his inspection of different schools, colleges, and charitable institutions, including Pestalozzi schools in Switzerland, in 1818 and 1819, was extensively noticed. Henry Barnard expressed the opinion that "no one volume of the first half of the nineteenth century had so wide an influence on the development of our educational, reformatory, and preventative measures, directly and indirectly as Griscom's book."[3]

Barnard himself was a major voice in spreading the Pestalozzian doctrines in America, becoming the most active of Pestalozzians, though his first visit to Europe did not occur until after Pestalozzi's death. Among his multifarious services to American education, Barnard edited the *Connecticut Common School Journal* from 1838 to 1842 and the *American Journal of Education* from 1856 to 1881. In using these organs to win support for the establishment of the common school he also popularized Pestalozzianism. Further, while conducting teachers' institutes Barnard presented lectures on Pestalozzi's educational theories and practices. His articles on the method and translated selections from Pestalozzi's writings were collected in his book *Pestalozzi and Pestalozzianism* (Syracuse, 1859), for many years the most widely used handbook on the subject in English.

A highly influential propagandist for the Pestalozzian doctrines in the United States was another European traveler, Horace Mann. Mann's account of the German school methods in his

Seventh Annual Report (1843) described in glowing terms the success of the Prussian-Pestalozzian system of education and urged American reforms along similar lines. The report created a sensation and was bitterly attacked by a group of thirty-one Boston schoolmasters and other conservatives throughout the country. Despite such diehard opposition, the proposed reforms were largely adopted under the leadership of Mann and his successors in the secretaryship of the Massachusetts State Board of Education.

Individual teachers also built on Pestalozzian foundations. Warren Colburn in 1821 published his *First Lessons in Arithmetic,* "on the plan of Pestalozzi, with some improvements." This text spread the "mental arithmetic" method throughout the country, bringing about a general reform of mathematics teaching in American schools. Lowell Mason, under the influence of Nägeli and inspired by William C. Woodbridge, made the teaching of music by Pestalozzian methods a permanent feature of American school curricula. Emma Willard and Woodbridge wrote two geography texts, following Pestalozzian principles, which effected a revolution in the teaching of that subject. Bronson Alcott and his brother advocated and practiced Pestalozzian ideas in their schools in Massachusetts; a "natural" system of instruction was introduced by them, adapted to the needs of the children, corporal punishment was eliminated, and the children were granted full freedom of expression. The Pestalozzian spirit was also brought to New England from Switzerland by Louis Agassiz and Arnold Guyot, who employed the general method in their study and teaching of natural history and geography.

According to George Sewell Boutwell, who followed Horace Mann as Secretary of the State Board of Education of Massachusetts, in at least four Massachusetts normal schools prior to 1860—Framingham, Westfield, Bridgewater, and Salem—"the art of teaching was taught according to the system of Pestalozzi and by well informed teachers and professors, and with the knowledge that it was the system of Pestalozzi"; and furthermore, "previous to 1859 the art of teaching according to the system of Pestalozzi had been taught and the practice of the art had been illustrated to thousands of students in the normal schools and to teachers in the teachers' institutes in the state of Massachusetts."[4]

In what has been described as a kind of second generation Pestalozzianism, there began in the 1860's the development of the "Oswego movement," which had wide influence in improving American education. The moving spirit was Edward A. Sheldon, superintendent of the Oswego, New York, schools. Sheldon determined that the principles of Pestalozzi would be introduced into the Oswego schools, and in 1861 he sent to the Home and Colonial Society in London for an experienced Pestalozzian to train his teachers in these methods. Margaret E. M. Jones and Hermann Krüsi, Jr., who were brought over, worked for many years in the Gray's Inn Road Training School, later one of the New York state normal schools, from which Pestalozzianism spread thoughout the country.

Concerning the Oswego movement, Sheldon wrote:

The system which we have adopted is justly termed Pestalozzian, for to Pestalozzi, that greatest of all modern reformers in education, may be credited the development and in many important points the origin of those ideas which lie at the basis of this system. It is true that these ideas, and the modes of applying them in the developement of the human faculties, have been somewhat modified and improved during the experience of half a century, but they are none the less the real thoughts and discoveries of this great philosopher. Its principles have become more or less widely diffused, but have been more generally and thoroughly incorporated with the methods of teaching in some of the countries of Europe than in our own.[5]

The basic operating principle at Oswego was that all knowledge derived from sense perception and all instruction should be based on real objects—a rather narrow interpretation of Pestalozzi's teachings. As stated by Sheldon and his associates when the Oswego program was inaugurated there in 1861, three central ideas predominated: first, all education should be according to the natural order of development of the human faculties; second, all knowledge is derived in the first instance from the perceptions of the senses, and therefore all instruction should be based upon real objects and occurrences; and third, the object of primary education is to give a harmonious cultivation to the faculties of the mind, and not to communicate technical knowledge. Materials and methods of instruction based on Pestalozzian principles used in Oswego were widely advertised, popularized, and imitated.

Although the Oswego movement greatly contributed to making Pestalozzi's name known to the American educational world, the method taught restricted the teaching of school subjects to the observation of natural objects. Sheldon published books of lesson plans based on the sensory examination of a number of common objects. In some instances, the object teaching was highly formalized and systematized. At Oswego, collections of materials used in physics, chemistry, botany, zoology, and mineralogy were placed before the children, who were required to describe them in scientific terms. The lessons on glass, water, and coal used a prestructured question and answer approach.

One conspicuous result of the Oswego plan was to subordinate book study. A delegation of prominent educators who visited the institution in 1862 observed that "the system substitutes in great measure teachers for the book," largely eliminating books from the primary schools. The consequences were that the teacher became an active instructor of groups of children, instead of a hearer of individual recitations; and children were given training in oral expression, which previously had practically no place in elementary schools.

So great was the interest in the Oswego program that the National Teachers Association meeting in Chicago in 1863 appointed a committee to investigate the principles of object teaching in general and the Oswego system in particular. The committee's report, submitted at a meeting of the Association at Harrisburg in 1865, concluded that "whenever this system has been confined to elementary instruction and has been employed by skillful, thorough teachers, in unfolding and disciplining the faculties, in fixing the attention and awakening thought, it has been successful. Pupils trained under this system have evinced more quickness and accuracy of perception, careful observation, and a correctness of judgement which results from accurate discrimination, and proper comparison. They have seemed much better acquainted with the works of nature, and better able to understand allusions to nature, art, and social life."[6] The committee proceeded, however, to warn against object lessons replacing the use of books in higher instruction.

Another significant American development inspired by Pestalozzian theories occurred in St. Louis, shortly after the Oswego movement began. William T. Harris, superintendent of the St.

Louis public schools from 1868 to 1880, was responsible for introducing object teaching in the field of natural science into the curriculum. The study of science was included in all grades of the district schools. In the first school year, instruction was given in botany, and the material covered the structure, color, perfume, habits, and shapes of flowers; the shape, uses, sap, and decay of leaves, fruits, and seeds; buds and roots, stalks and trunks, bark of plants and wood; circulation of sap, uses of sap, and sleep of plants. During the second year, animal study, with special reference to physiology, was taken up, followed in the third year by the elements of physical nature—air, wind, water, and gravitation. The fourth and fifth years were devoted to fuller and more systematic study of zoology, physiology, and hygiene. Physical geography was introduced in the sixth year and elementary physics in the seventh year. A syllabus of lessons on natural science prepared by Harris for the use of St. Louis teachers was widely reprinted by school superintendents elsewhere in the country.

In his first annual report as superintendent of the St. Louis schools, Harris discussed his views on Pestalozzianism and problems involved in object teaching. He noted that "Pestalozzi lived at a time when all Europe was done to death with formalism. . . . He began with the intention to elevate the natural over the spiritual; to dissolve the subject into the object rather than the contrary."[7] Harris was not blind, however, to the faults in Pestalozzi's method. One of the virtues of the St. Louis program of nature study was avoidance of the one-sided emphasis on sense perception frequently urged by advocates of object teaching and the Pestalozzian doctrine, though it recognized and utilized the distinct educational values in the system.

Pestalozzianism exerted its greatest influence in the United States during the last four decades of the nineteenth century. The Oswego movement led the way with its stress on the object teaching plan. The introduction of natural science into the St. Louis schools soon led to the incorporation of some form of natural science into the curriculum of common schools throughout the nation. Through these channels and others, Pestalozzian methods reached all parts of the country, leading eventually to improved schools and better training of teachers. The use of "object teaching" schemes in American schools became general.

More important still, the impact of Pestalozzian thought was felt
in spreading the concept of free public schools, first in New England and subsequently, after about 1840, in other states.

Among the major nineteenth-century advances in American
education that can be traced back to Pestalozzi are the minimiz-
ing or abolition of whipping and other cruel punishments; the
great lessening of rote memory, especially the memorizing of
words not understood; the introduction into the schools of music,
drawing, geography, science, and nature study; and the improvement of teaching and the professional preparation of
teachers.

The spirit of Pestalozzi has also been felt in the twentieth century. A recent writer, Gerald Lee Gutek, sums up the chief effects as follows: emphasis is being placed on the interests and
needs of the child, on child freedom based upon natural development, on direct experience with the world and its activities,
on the use of the senses in training pupils in observation and
judgment, and on cooperation between the school and home and
between parents and teachers.[8] A close kinship exists also between the philosophies of Pestalozzi and such educators as John
Dewey, who urged that all learning should originate in the
learner's experience; and William Heard Kilpatrick, who condemned excessive bookishness, verbalism, and memorization, and
all that was purely abstract and theoretical.

CHAPTER 12

Afterword

A S the eighteenth century drew to a close, teaching methods were scarcely distinguishable from those that prevailed in Ptolemy's day. At ancient Alexandria, in the third century B.C., the principle had been established that the school's purpose is to teach the written word, and this dogmatic belief remained fixed for the next two thousand years. Profound changes in that concept and the modern era in education date from the advent in Switzerland of Johann Heinrich Pestalozzi during the last quarter of the eighteenth century.

Prior to Pestalozzi's appearance on the scene, the process of teaching, essentially, was to require pupils to memorize words—a process almost invariably accompanied by unmerciful punishments. The children came to associate learning with nothing except constant floggings and hatred of their teachers. On their part, the teachers were simply accepting the popular conviction that children are innately bad and antagonistic to learning and that the rod was the only device for reforming their erroneous attitudes.

From Pestalozzi's point of view, the most deplorable aspects of the prevailing system were the practical exclusion of the poorest children from education, the "superficial verbosity," as he termed it, of pupil recitation, and the cruel custom of corporal punishment of children who failed. Pestalozzi's principles, as they developed, were based upon the education of the common people as well as the rich, the kindly treatment of children, and his own concepts of the psychology of children and of learning. All these doctrines were in opposition to the evils, as he saw them, of current educational practices.

The original inspiration for Pestalozzi's choice of an educational career appears to have come from the reading of Jean Jacques Rousseau's *Emile*, describing the education from birth to manhood of an imaginary boy. Following Rousseau's lead, Pestalozzi rejected religious aims and the teaching of mere words and facts, which had previously characterized all elementary education, and tried to establish the educational process according to a well-organized routine, based on what he considered to be the natural and orderly development of the instincts, capacities, and powers of the growing child. Rousseau's idea of a return to nature was applied to education. Accordingly, Pestalozzi rejected what he described as the "empty chattering of mere words," and "outward show" in the instruction in reading and the catechism, and replaced them with studies based on observation, experimentation, and reasoning. Sense impression became the watchword; therefore, read nothing, discover everything, and prove all things.

At the time of Pestalozzi's birth in mid-eighteenth century, the caste system was solidly established in Switzerland and indeed throughout Europe. A small aristocracy at the top ruled through wealth and literacy, while the masses, who supported the owners of the land in idleness and luxury, were sunk in ignorance, poverty, and vice. Schools for the common people were few, the content of education was largely limited by ecclesiastical authority, and the methods, as noted, were traditional and verbal. The teachers generally had little training and were selected with slight regard for their qualifications. Frequently, they were old soldiers, workmen, or tradesmen who stood over the children while the latter picked up a few rudiments of learning.

A review of the highlights of the life of the man who was destined to exert immense influence in changing existing conditions reveals the motivations and forces which drove him. Pestalozzi grew up in his native town of Zurich. His social consciousness emerged early in the activities of a group of young men, the "Patriots," who tried to improve their community's civic life. After foregoing dreams of entering the ministry or the legal profession, Pestalozzi became a farmer. His plan to cultivate madder at Neuhof, "New Farm," was a dismal failure, leaving him and his family in poverty. Undeterred by that calamity, he opened a school for the children of poor farmers and various waifs and strays with a kind of home-industrial program, to teach the children how to earn their living without risk of starvation or of becoming chronic beggars. The period was opportune, for Switzerland was then in transition from agriculture to domestic industry.

Pestalozzi's thought, basically, was that a country life, in which the cultivation of land was combined with some sort of handicraft, would provide the best means of teaching the poorest children. Instruction included practical farm work, household chores, and spinning and weaving, along with elementary lessons in reading, writing, and arithmetic. For the firsthand study of nature, the children were taken on long walks through the neighboring valleys. There was no memorizing or flogging. Educationally, the enterprise was successful, but it had to be abandoned after a few years because of lack of financial support. The shock of the second failure broke the health of Pestalozzi's wife, who until then had been a loyal companion and helpmate.

For approximately the next twenty years, Pestalozzi gave up further educational experiments, but not his deep and abiding interest in the field. To spread the message he felt he had for the world, and to ease his frustrations, he turned to writing. His basic theories of education were outlined for the first time in a series of aphorisms entitled *The Evening Hours of a Hermit*, wherein the doctrine is set forth that human life grows in concentric circles, beginning with the family, followed by the "personal sphere" (work or profession), and finally by the third, state and country. If these circles develop in natural fashion, the individual leads a satisfying life. The purpose of education, according to Pestalozzi, should be to make certain that the organic growth is undisturbed.

In his next major work, *Leonard and Gertrude*, Pestalozzi pays particular attention to family education, especially the key role played by the mother, Gertrude, whose common sense and sound judgment concerning education influence first her family, then her village, and finally the state. Here and elsewhere in his writings and in his own career, Pestalozzi pays warm tribute to the women who played important parts in his life and work.

Pestalozzi's chief concern always was the common people. As a remedy for poverty and want, "to stop the sources of misery," he never lost faith in education. The poor must be educated to help themselves. Pestalozzi's next opportunity to aid deprived children came in the war that followed the French Revolution. By delegation from the Swiss government, in 1799, he took over Stans Castle, and struggled almost alone to save dozens of children left orphans or destitute in the wake of the fighting. The heroic attempt ended prematurely when the castle was preempted for military purposes. For the third time, Pestalozzi was faced with failure.

Shortly thereafter Pestalozzi initiated one of his major educational experiments, at Burgdorf, 1799-1804, an institution that contributed much to his growing fame. Special teaching methods developed during that period were explained by Pestalozzi in his most important pedagogical work, *How Gertrude Teaches Her Children*, In which he presents his educational principles. The theories were put into practice first at Burgdorf and later at Müchenbuchsee and at Yverdon. They were designed to guide children as they progressed from elementary stages to the more complicated, from simple observation to understanding. The "path of nature" in learning, according to Pestalozzi, was a combination of three elements: form, number, and word, each step building upon the previous one and all based on personal experience. Empty wordiness was discouraged.

Pestalozzi's last educational venture of any consequence was at Yverdon, over a twenty-year period, 1805-1825, a continuation of the program begun at Burgdorf. The school at Yverdon comprised elementary and classical courses, industrial training for boys and girls, and the preparation of teachers. A number of nationalities were represented among the pupils and distinguished visitors came from all over Europe and even from America to become acquainted with the celebrated Swiss institution. A project that received much attention, both at Burgdorf and Yverdon, was the designing of objects to use in teaching language, geography, arithmetic, and science. Textbooks were written and the Pestalozzian methods were spread further by teachers from Switzerland and abroad who had gone through the preparatory curriculum.

A basic principle in Pestalozzi's teaching, as previously noted, was that learning is best accomplished through experience, observation, and the handling of actual objects, rather than by precept, books, or blind memorization. "Either we go from words to things," he wrote, "or from things to words."[1] He insisted upon starting with things. The knowledge of geography and geology could most profitably be acquired by observing natural phenomena; numbers, by counting objects; letters, by manipulating alphabet blocks; and fractions, by calculating from squares cut up into halves, thirds, and quarters.

One of the consequences of the Pestalozzian ideas was a considerable expansion of the curriculum. In addition to traditional
subjects, the children in his schools were taught singing, drawing, pasteboard modeling, gardening, natural history, the study of
rocks, "mental arithmetic," and geography. Lessons were presented orally—but not for memorization; reading was taught by
the word method instead of by use of the alphabet; and definite
efforts were made to stir and to maintain the interest of the
pupils. The child was viewed as "a little seed" containing the design of the mature tree, and Pestalozzi was convinced that a
"gradual imperceptible advance" was "nature's way" in a child's
education.

Although he became famous in his later years, Pestalozzi was
never fully satisfied. He felt that he had abandoned his lifelong
ambition to educate the poor, to establish the idea of family education. Instead, he was operating boarding schools for wealthy
children. Toward the end of his life he founded an orphanage
from the proceeds of his literary works. Once more, however, financial troubles intervened, and after a short time the school for
the poor was merged with the Yverdon institution.

As he approached the end of his career, Pestalozzi met with
further disappointments. Bitter differences of opinion developed
among his associates at Yverdon, and in effect he lost control of
his own creation. Pestalozzi's writings and speeches in his old age
reflect his frustrations, which seem to have caused him to forget
his own great achievements. Never, however, did Pestalozzi lose
his faith in his educational credo or his long-range optimism.
These are reflected in his final writings, *Addresses to His House*
and *Swan Song*. His belief in the power of education to regener-
ate society seldom if ever faltered. From start to finish, his work
was concerned with trying to "teach beggars to live like men."

In the application of his principles of education, Pestalozzi was
often inconsistent; in fact, it has been remarked that his method
consisted in having no method. The unrivaled incapacity for governing any kind of enterprise, to which he confessed, extended to
any kind of orderly presentation of his theories and their practice.
Yet, despite such drawbacks, Pestalozzi must be assigned a high
rank among teachers. He possessed a remarkable instinct for developing the faculties of his pupils. To set the intellectual
machinery in motion, to make it work and keep it working, was

the prime object. In reaching that aim, Pestalozzi relied upon an essential principle in education: to arouse the thorough interest of his pupils in the lesson, mainly through their own direct participation. He influenced the children to concentrate all their powers upon the subject at hand. Whatever Pestalozzi's teaching may have lacked, it was intensely interesting to the children and made them love learning. His conception of the teacher's function was preeminently to stir up the pupil's energies and thereby bring about his self-development. The teacher becomes the stimulator and director of the intellectual processes by which the learner educates himself. To Pestalozzi, self-education is the only genuine education.

Beyond all educators who preceded him, Pestalozzi attached paramount importance to the elementary stages of teaching. Elementary education, in his view, meant not so much definite instruction in special subjects but the preparation of the pupil's mind—the all-sided development of its powers—for more advanced instruction and learning. The Pestalozzian precept for the teacher was always to begin the pupil's education by dealing with concrete things and facts, and not with such abstractions and generalizations as definitions, rules, and simply words.

Pestalozzi's own estimate of his contribution to the field of elementary education is contained in this statement: "If I look back and ask myself what I have really done towards the improvement of elementary education, I find that in recognizing observation [Anschauung] as the absolute basis of all knowledge, I have established the first and most important principle of instruction; and that, setting aside all particular systems, I have endeavored to discover what ought to be the character of instruction itself, and what are the fundamental laws according to which the natural education of the human race must be conducted."[2] Elsewhere he adds, "Observation is the absolute basis of all knowledge. In other words, all knowledge must proceed from observation, and must admit of being traced to that source."[3]

The principle of Anschauung, according to Pestalozzi, can be made effective only by educating the learner's senses and making him an accurate observer. The habit of accurate observation is not taught by nature, but must be acquired by experience. Pestalozzi's doctrine, then, was that all elementary instruction must begin with the near, the real, the concrete, and never in the case of young children with the remote, the abstract, and the ideal, never with definitions, generalities, or rules, unsupported by direct observation.

Based on the results of his educational experiments, further elaborating this concept, Pestalozzi declared: "There unfolded itself gradually in my mind the idea of an ABC of observation to which I now attach great importance and in the working out of which the whole scheme of a general method of instruction in all its scope appeared, though still obscure, before my eyes."[4] An important principle was to reduce all subject matter to its simplest elements and to adopt observation of these elements to the level of the child's development. Sense-perception was held by Pestalozzi to be the starting point of thought, that is, the direct impression produced on the internal and external senses by the world around us. A child's first ideas are derived from these impressions, and they inspire in him the desire to express his thoughts by signs, and later in words. Sense-perception or observation, following this principle, is the foundation of instruction, but must be joined by expression in language, since clear and exact impressions must form the basis for clear and exact speech.

A special difficulty that confronted Pestalozzi—incidentally, a problem usually ignored by his critics—was that he had to deal not only with children of different ages and social groups, but also with children who spoke different dialects or even different languages. Methods of teaching had to be devised by Pestalozzi to surmount this obstacle to learning.

Tributes to Pestalozzi by distinguished contemporaries and later writers are innumerable. Karl von Raumer, for example, notes that "he compelled the scholastic world to revise the whole of their task, to reflect on the nature and destiny of man, as also on the proper way of leading him from his youth towards his destiny."[5] Johann Fichte wrote, "Pestalozzi's essential aim has been to raise the lower classes, and clear away all differences between them and the educated classes. It is not only popular education that is thus realized, but national education."[6] Herbart commented that "the whole field of actual and possible sense-perception is open to the Pestalozzian method. . . . The Pestalozzian method is by no means qualified to crowd out any other method, but to prepare the way for it. It takes the earliest age that is at all capable of receiving instruction. It treats it with the

seriousness and simplicity which are appropriate where the very
first raw materials are to be procured."[7] In his *History of
Education,* Thomas Davidson adds, "Pestalozzi is the parent of
the modern love for children, and it is this love that has trans-
formed education from a harsh repressive discipline into a tender,
thoughtful guidance. . . . After Pestalozzi people saw children
with new eyes, invested them with new interest, and felt the importance of placing them in a true relation to the world of nature
and culture. It is not too much to say that all modern education
breathes the spirit of Pestalozzi. It is education for freedom, not
for subordination."[8] Finally, W. C. Woodbridge, in the *Annals of
Education,* sums up the case in eloquent terms: "Pestalozzi com-
bated with unshrinking boldness and untiring perseverance,
through a long life, the prejudices and abuses of the age in reference to education, both by his example and by his numerous
publications. He attacked with great vigour, and no small degree
of success, that favourite maxim of bigotry and tyranny, that
obedience and devotion are the legitimate offspring of ignorance.
. . . In this way he produced an impulse which pervaded Europe
and which, by means of his popular and theoretical works,
reached the cottages of the poor and the palaces of the great."[9]

Pestalozzi's major achievements, briefly stated, were these: he
forced education to be democratic, he introduced psychology into
education, he revolutionized teaching methods, he was a leader
in research and experimentation in education, and he introduced
the concept of child study, by insisting that the child must be
treated as a living and growing organism. Pestalozzi must be recognized as the first person who attempted to analyze and to sys-
tematize the elements of the science of education.

Perhaps Pestalozzi's greatest influence was exerted through his
disciples, particularly by way of such individuals as Fichte,
Fröbel, and Herbart. Through these men, in various ways,
Pestalozzi's ideas eventually helped to shape all modern education.

Walch's study of Pestalozzi points out that some of the most
basic Pestalozzian principles are of ancient origin. The idea, for
example, that all knowledge must be based on sense experience
goes back to Aristotle and was an essential element in the educational theories of Comenius (1592-1670) and Basedow (1724-1790).
The importance of early home training has been stressed

throughout the history of education, by Quintilian, Saint John Chrysostom, and numerous other writers. Another Pestalozzian thought, constantly emphasized, that education should be a harmonious development of the physical, intellectual, and moral powers can be traced back to the ancient Athenian ideal of the education of the "perfect man."[10] Conceding the validity of these findings, it is nevertheless true that Pestalozzi revitalized the conceptions noted, giving them new life and currency, as well as gaining for them general acceptance.

In the practical application of such principles, too, Pestalozzi rates as a pioneer. The study of psychology in its modern sense had scarcely begun in his era. He was forced to depend, therefore, on intuition, controlled by logic and judgment.

The Swiss reformer's influence outside his own country was widespread throughout the nineteenth century. Historically, the greatest single effect of Pestalozzi's teachings was on the German educational system. Horace Mann and other American educators visiting Europe prior to the Civil War returned home vastly impressed by their observations of the German and Swiss schools. The great reform of American education during the 1830-1860 period was inspired directly or indirectly by Pestalozzi.

Kate Silber, Pestalozzi's principal modern biographer, concludes: "What enabled Pestalozzi always to recover from despondency and gave him strength in the most adverse circumstances were his love and his faith. He was deeply religious in the immanent sense of religion: he believed in the Divine in every human being, however neglected, and his untiring efforts were directed towards helping it to life. His enterprises may not have been successful and his writings difficult to read, yet there still remains in them a strong appeal for helpfulness and loving kindness, which are as important and needful to-day as ever."[11]

Notes and References

Chapter One

1. J. A. Green, *The Educational Ideas of Pestalozzi* (N.Y., 1969), p. 13. (Originally published in 1914)
2. Henry Holman, *Pestalozzi: An Account of His Life and Work.* (N.Y., 1908), pp. 23-24.
3. Green, *op. cit.*, p. 13.
4. Gerald Lee Gutek, *Pestalozzi & Education* (N.Y., 1968), pp. 101-02.
5. Henry Barnard, *Pestalozzi and His Educational System* (Syracuse, N.Y., 1874), p. 667.
6. Gutek, *op. cit.*, p. 104.
7. Holman, *op. cit.*, pp. 28-29.

Chapter Two

1. Auguste Pinloche, *Pestalozzi and the Foundation of the Modern Elementary School* (N.Y., 1901), pp. 3-4.
2. Holman, *op. cit.*, p. 20.
3. Sr. Mary Romana Walch, *Pestalozzi and the Pestalozzian Theory of Education* (Washington, D.C., 1952), pp. 3-4.
4. Roger de Guimps, *Pestalozzi, His Life and Work* (N.Y. 1901), p. 5.
5. Gustav E. Mueller, "Heinrich Pestalozzi—His Life and Work," *Harvard Educational Review*, 16 (1946), 142.
6. Holman, *op. cit.*, p. 23.
7. Guimps, *op. cit.*, p. 6.
8. Holman, *op. cit.*, p. 27.
9. Pinloche, *op. cit.*, p. 11.
10. *Ibid.*, p. 11.
11. *Ibid.*, pp. 11-12.
12. Michael Heafford, *His Thought and His Relevance* (London, 1967), p. 9.
13. *Ibid.*, pp. 9-10.
14. *Ibid.*, pp. 10-11.

15. *Ibid.*, p. 11.
16. Pinloche, *op cit.*, p. 125.
17. Heafford, *op. cit.*, p. 11.
18. Holman, *op. cit.*, p. 48.

Chapter Three

1. Green, *op. cit.*, p. 27.
2. Gutek, *op. cit.*, p. 33.
3. Holman, *op. cit.*, p. 54.
4. *Ibid.*, p. 56.
5. *Ibid.*, p. 58.
6. Kate Silber, *Pestalozzi, the Man and his Work* (London, 1960), p. 48.
7. Silber, *op. cit.*, p. 48.
8. Guimps, *op. cit.*, p. 106.
9. *Ibid.*, p. 111.
10. *Ibid.*, p. 111.
11. Mueller, *op. cit.*, p. 148.
12. Silber, *op. cit.*, p. 103.
13. Heafford, *op. cit.*, p. 14.
14. *Ibid.*, p. 26.
15. Pinloche, *op. cit.*, p. 125.
16. Guimps, *op. cit.*, pp. 368-69.
17. *Ibid.*, p. 369.

Chapter Four

1. Pinloche, *op. cit.*, p. 32.
2. Silber, *op. cit.*, p. 112.
3. Guimps, *op. cit.*, pp. 133-34.
4. Holman, *op. cit.*, p. 73.
5. *Ibid.*, pp. 73-74.
6. Heafford, *op cit.*, p. 20.
7. Guimps, *op. cit.*, p. 137.
8. Pinloche, *op. cit.*, pp. 33-34.
9. Holman, *op. cit.*, p. 78.
10. Heafford, *op. cit.*, p. 20.
11. Green, *op. cit.*, p. 44.
12. Guimps, *op. cit.*, p. 174.
13. Guimps, *op. cit.*, p. 174.
14. R. Bigler, *Pestalozzi in Burgdorf* (Logan, Utah, 1972), p. 20.
15. Guimps, *op. cit.*, p. 176.
16. *Ibid.*, pp. 177-78.
17. *Ibid.*, p. 187.
18. *Ibid.*, p. 214.

19. *Silber, op. cit.,* p. 157.

Chapter Five

1. Herman Krüsi, *Pestalozzi: His Life, Work and Influence* (Cincinnati, 1875), p. 169.
2. Barnard, *op. cit.,* p. 699.
3. Walch, *op. cit.,* p. 135.
4. Holman, *op. cit.,* pp. 223-24.
5. *Ibid.,* p. 226.
6. Walch, *op. cit.,* p. 136.
7. *Ibid.,* p. 136.
8. *Ibid.,* p. 128.
9. Holman, *op. cit.,* pp. 230-31.
10. Walch, *op. cit.,* p. 126.
11. Guimps, *op. cit.,* pp. 390.
12. Krüsi, *op. cit.,* p. 178.
13. Walch, *op. cit.,* p. 131.
14. *Ibid.,* pp. 131-32.
15. Holman, *op. cit.,* p. 236.
16. "Pestalozzi and the Teaching of Science," *Nature,* 119 (1927), 378.
17. Krüsi, *op. cit.,* p. 178.
18. *Ibid.,* pp. 178-79.
19. *Ibid.,* p. 179.
20. Holman, *op. cit.,* p. 238.
21. *Ibid,* p. 238.
22. Krüsi, *op. cit.,* p. 175.
23. Holman, *op. cit.,* p. 216.
24. Krüsi, *op. cit.,* p. 176.
25. Holman, *op. cit.,* pp. 215-16.
26. *Ibid.,* p. 217.
27. *Ibid.,* p. 218.
28. Walch, *op. cit.,* p. 134.
29. Holman, *op. cit.,* p. 220.
30. Heafford, *op. cit.,* p. 54.
31. Holman, *op. cit.,* p. 246.
32. *Ibid.,* p. 247.
33. Heafford, *op. cit.,* p. 67.
34. Walch, *op. cit.,* p. 142.
35. Guimps, *op. cit.,* p. 271.
36. Green, *op. cit.,* p. 128.
37. *Ibid.,* p. 128.
38. Gutek, *op. cit.,* p. 147.
39. Walch, *op. cit.,* pp. 143-44.
40. Krüsi, *op. cit.,* p. 179.

Chapter Six

1. Silber, *op. cit.*, p. 206.
2. Krüsi, *op. cit.*, p. 45.
3. *Ibid.*, p. 46.
4. Pinloche, *op. cit.*, p. 68.
5. Holman, *op. cit.*, p. 96.
6. Krüsi, *op. cit.*, p. 49.
7. Pinloche, *op. cit.*, pp. 73-74.
8. Holman, *op. cit.*, p. 104.
9. Pinloche, *op. cit.*, p. 100.
10. Silber, *op. cit.*, p. 130.
11. Pinloche, *op. cit.*, p. 83.
12. *Ibid.*, p. 83.
13. Guimps, *op. cit.*, p. 253.
14. Pinloche, *op. cit.*, p. 85.
15. Holman, *op. cit.*, p. 109.
16. Heafford, *op. cit.*, p. 32.
17. Holman, *op. cit.*, p. 110.
18. *Ibid.*, p. 111.
19. Heafford, *op. cit.*, p. 33.
20. *Ibid.*, p. 35.

Chapter Seven

1. Barnard, *op. cit.*, p. 510.
2. Barnard, *op. cit.*, p. 511.
3. Frank P. Graves, *Great Educators of Three Centuries.* (N.Y., 1912), p. 144.
4. Graves, *op. cit.*, p. 144.
5. *Ibid.*, p. 145.
6. *Ibid.*, p. 145.
7. Barnard, *op. cit.*, p. 715.
8. Silber, *op. cit.*, p. 28.
9. Heafford, *op. cit.*, p. 76.
10. Green, *op. cit.*, p. 79.
11. *Ibid.*, pp. 94-95.
12. Gabriel Compayré, *Pestalozzi and Elementary Education* (N.Y., 1907), p. 72.
13. Heafford, *op. cit.*, p. 44.
14. Paul Monroe, ed., *Encyclopedia of Education* (N.Y., 1914), v. 4, p. 658.
15. *Ibid.*, p. 658.
16. Krüsi, *op. cit.*, p. 152.
17. *Ibid.*, p. 187.
18. *Ibid.*, p. 192.

19. Green, *op. cit.*, pp. 189-90.
20. Barnard, *op. cit.*, p. 505.
21. Holman, *op. cit.*, p. 261.
22. *Ibid.*, p. 262.
23. *Ibid.*, p. 269.
24. *Ibid.*, pp. 269-70.

Chapter Eight

1. Green, *op. cit.*, pp. 70-71.
2. *Ibid.*, p. 69.
3. *Holman, op. cit.*, p. 150.
4. *Ibid.*, p. 154.
5. *Yearbook of Education*, 1963 (N.Y., 1963), p. 68.
6. *Ibid.*, p. 68.
7. Tadasu Misawa, *Modern Educators and Their Ideals* (N.Y., 1909), 138-39.
8. Silber, *op. cit.*, p. 87.
9. *Ibid.*, p. 84.

Chapter Nine

1. Green, *op. cit.*, p. 132.
2. *Ibid.*, p. 132.
3. *Ibid.*, p. 133.
4. Holman, *op. cit.*, p. 250.
5. T. F. Kinloch, *Pioneers of Religious Education* (London, 1939), p. 98.
6. Silber, *op. cit.*, p. 174.
7. Kinloch, *op. cit.*, p. 91-92.
8. *Ibid.*, p. 92.
9. Green, *op. cit.*, 136.
10. *Ibid.*, p. 137.
11. Holman, *op. cit.*, p. 255.
12. Green, *op. cit.*, p. 146.
13. Silber, *op. cit.*, p. 184.
14. Green, *op. cit.*, p. 150.

Chapter Ten

1. Green, *op. cit.*, p. 166.
2. Barnard, *op. cit.*, p. 146.
3. Krüsi, *op. cit.*, p. 208.
4. Holman, *op. cit.*, p. 308.
5. *Ibid.*, p. 308.
6. *Ibid.*, p. 308.
7. Green, *op. cit.*, p. 171.

8. Krüsi *op. cit.*, p. 210.
9. *Ibid.*, p. 215.
10. *Ibid.*, pp. 217-18.
11. Karl von Raumer, *The Life and System of Pestalozzi* (London, 1855), p. 66.
12. Compayré, *op. cit.*, p. 107.
13. Silber, *op. cit.*, p. 290.
14. *Ibid.*, p. 296.
15. *Ibid.*, p. 298.
16. Gutek, *op. cit.*, pp. 159-60.
17. Silber, *op. cit.*, p. 304.

Chapter Eleven

1. Gutek, *op. cit.*, pp. 161-62.
2. Will S. Monroe, *History of the Pestalozzian Movement in the United States* (Syracuse, N.Y., 1907), pp. 51-52.
3. Barnard, *op. cit.*, p. 399.
4. Will S. Monroe, *op. cit.*, p. 136.
5. *Ibid.*, p. 176.
6. *Ibid.*, pp. 183-184.
7. *Ibid.*, p. 201.
8. Gutek, *op. cit.*, p. 165.

Chapter Twelve

1. Holman, *op. cit.*, p. 198.
2. *Ibid.*, pp. 180-81.
3. *Ibid.*, p. 181.
4. Graves, *op. cit.*, p. 133.
5. Holman, *op. cit.*, p. 307.
6. *Ibid.*, p. 308.
7. *Ibid.*, p. 308.
8. *Ibid.*, p. 309.
9. *Ibid.*, p. 310.
10. Walch, *op. cit.*, pp. 166-67.
11. *Journal of Education* (London), 78 (1946), 250.

Selected Bibliography

Four collected editions of Pestalozzi's writings have been published, all in German, under the title *Sämtliche Werke:* Stuttgart and Tübingen, 1819-26. 15 v.; Brandenburg, 1869-73. 18 v.; Liegnitz, 1899-1902. 12 v.; Berlin, Leipzig, and Zurich, 1927-64. 21 v. A collected edition has also been issued in Japanese, but none in English. In 1912, J. A. Green edited and published in London a one-volume work, *Pestalozzi's Educational Writings.* Otherwise, only selected individual titles have been translated into English. *British Books in Print* records nothing currently in print, and the American *Books in Print* lists only three titles by Pestalozzi: *Education of Man, Aphorisms* (Westport, Conn.: Greenwood Press) and *How Gertrude Teaches Her Children* and *How Mothers Teach Their Children* (N.Y.: Gordon Press).

BARNARD, HENRY. *Pestalozzi and His Educational System.* Syracuse, N.Y.: C. W. Bardeen, 1874.

BIBER, EDUARD. *Henry Pestalozzi and His Plan of Education.* London: Sauter, 1831.

BIGLER, R. *Pestalozzi in Burgdorf.* Logan: Utah State University Press, 1972.

COMPAYRÉ, GABRIEL. *Pestalozzi and Elementary Education.* N.Y.: Crowell, 1907.

GRAVES, FRANK P. *Great Educators of Three Centuries.* N.Y.: Macmillan, 1912. pp. 122-66.

GREEN, J. A. *The Educational Ideas of Pestalozzi.* N.Y.: Greenwood Press, 1969. (Originally published in 1914).

GUIMPS, ROGER DE. *Pestalozzi, His Life and Work.* N.Y.: Appleton, 1901.

GUTEK, GERALD LEE. *Pestalozzi and Education.* N.Y.: Random House, 1968.

HAYWARD, F. H. *The Educational Ideas of Pestalozzi and Fròbel.* London: Ralph Holland, 1905.

HEAFFORD, MICHAEL. *Pestalozzi, His Thought and Its Relevance Today.* London: Methuen, 1967.

HOLMAN, HENRY. *Pestalozzi: An Account of His Life and Work.* N.Y.: Longmans, Green, 1908.

KRÜSI, HERMANN. *Pestalozzi: His Life, Work, and Influence.* Cincinnati: Wilson, Hinkle & Co., 1875.

MONROE, WILL S. *History of the Pestalozzian Movement in the United States.* Syracuse, N.Y.: C. W. Bardeen, 1907.

MUELLER, GUSTAV E. "Heinrich Pestalozzi: His Life and Work." *Harvard Educational Review*, 16 (1946), 141-59.

PESTALOZZI, HEINRICH. *Letters on Early Education Addressed to J. P. Greaves*, Syracuse, N.Y.: C. W. Bardeen, 1898.

Pestalozzi and His Times, a Pictorial Record. Ed. by Pestalozzianum and the Zentralbibliothek Zurich. N.Y.: Stechert, 1928.

PINCLOCHE, AUGUSTE. *Pestalozzi and the Foundation of the Modern Elementary School.* N.Y.: Scribner, 1901.

SILBER, KATE. *Pestalozzi, the Man and His Work.* London: Routledge, 1960. 2d ed., 1965.

WALCH, SR. MARY ROMANA. *Pestalozzi and the Pestalozzian Theory of Education.* Wash., D.C.: Catholic Univ. of America Press, 1952.

Index

145